State of the game or game of the state?

> THE CHILEAN junta, faced with a visit next week from two observers from FIFA, are attempting to put their house in superficial enough order to ensure that Chile's crucial World Cup qualifying match will be played on November 21 in Santiago. From the Chilean capital our correspondent Florencia Varas reports:
> "The FIFA commission will check on local conditions, particularly the state of the national stadium which, since the coup, has been used to house several thousand arrested political prisoners.

'Some people talk about football as if it were life or death itself; but it's much more serious than that.'

So you think Bill Shankly, manager of Liverpool for fifteen years, was joking? The day before I wrote this sentence, around *one thousand million* people spent their Sunday afternoon in front of the television, watching the 1974 World Cup Final between Holland and West Germany. Fine entertainment for millions—but much more than that for some of the audience. Consider what different reactions we had from politicians, team managers and the general population following their players' performance at Munich:

Uruguay After the defeat that put them out of the competition, their manager stated: 'This is the worst football we have ever played. It is a national disgrace: we shall be publicly tried on our return.'

Brazil Following their defeat by Holland, attempts were made to burn down the house of the manager, Zagalo, and coffins for some of the once idolized players were paraded in the streets.

Haiti Ernst Jean-Josephe, a defender, who was found to have taken drugs before the match against Italy, was beaten up and sent home in disgrace on the orders of the Duvalier regime.

Italy After dodging a shower of tomatoes at Rome airport in 1966, the Italian team this time were attacked by 500 of their supporters as they left the stadium in Stuttgart, where Poland had ended their hopes of reaching the Final.

Holland Shortly after the final, the Dutch star Johan Cruyff was made a Knight of the Order of Orange Nassau, an award for those who 'have rendered special service to throne, state or society'.

Football is essentially a simple ball game open to anyone with legs, lungs and a bit of leather—or, these days, plastic. But can it still really be called a game? Or is it little more than a part of the world of business and politics?

Football means different things to different people: it can be something you're forced to do at school, a TV entertainment, a great way of spending Saturday afternoon with your mates, a chance of a job that is different—or a strange and stupid kind of nonsense that everyone but you gets worked up over. How did it come to have so many different faces?

Before and after the battle. Right: West Berlin police protect the Chilean team's hotel before the 1974 World Cup gets under way. Below: Johan Cruyff and Pleun Strik get their laurel wreaths on arrival back home, even though Holland lost 2–1 to West Germany in the Final.

Yesterday's men

'In the sense that democracy is intended to fulfil the will of the people, the survival of football has proved a triumph for democracy.' Percy M. Young, *A History of British Football*

At one level, football is still very much a neighbourhood affair. Every week something like two million players turn out for amateur teams, in local parks or on village pitches. Many more can be found kicking a ball around on the nearest patch of grass, chunk of waste land or not too busy street. At a time when attendances at League grounds are falling dramatically, more people than ever are turning to playing rather than watching the game. Indeed, it can be argued that the professional game is no more than a sophisticated, and well-publicized, digression from the mainstream of local contests.

If we look back at earlier versions of the game we can see the connection between park football on a Sunday today, and the fierce contests between opposing villages that continued well into the nineteenth century. If in those days they were less bothered about such matters as touchlines, free kicks or referees, there certainly seemed to be more scope for individual initiative than is possible in any version of today's game.

The traditional match between the two parishes of All Saints and St Peter's in Derby, for example, produced some interesting 'moves':

'The opposing parties endeavoured by every possible means, and by the exertion of their utmost strength, to carry the ball in the direction of their respective goals, and by this means the town was traversed and retraversed many times in the course of the day; indeed to such an extent has the contest been carried, that some years ago the fortunate holder of the ball, having made his way into the river Derwent, was followed by the whole body, who took to the water in the most gallant style, and kept up the chase to near the village of Duffield, a distance of five miles, the whole course being against the rapid stream, and one or two weirs having to be passed; on another occasion, the possessor of the ball is said to have quietly dropped himself into the culvert or sewer which passes under the town, and to have been followed by several others of both parties, and, after fighting his way the whole distance under the town, to have come out victorious at the other side where, a considerable party having collected, the contest was renewed in the river.'

In football games like this one played at Kingston on Thames in 1846, few could distinguish player from spectator. Today, the 2442 players who hire their pitches at Hackney Marshes on a Sunday morning have to be quite clear where their own game begins and ends.

'Bustling over large balls'

Of course football had been around a long time in one form or another before the Derby game took place in the middle of the nineteenth century. The ancient Greeks played a kind of football during their athletics and drama festivals. The Chinese emperor staged the game at his court, where the defeated team not only lost the match but also their heads. The Romans colonizing Britain, the Renaissance courtiers of Florence, the American Indians: all are on record as playing a brand of football. No doubt other societies have had a similar involvement, but haven't had anyone to record the fact. In Britain football seems to have been popular from the twelfth century on. For several hundred years it remained a vigorous and widespread folk sport, despite numerous attempts by judges, kings, queens and churchmen to ban the game, or to fine and imprison players.

Quite often during the eighteenth century, a football match was organized as a cover for other kinds of action. For instance, in 1765 in Northamptonshire many people were deprived of work and of the use of their land when the famous enclosure bill got through Parliament. People in the village of West Haddon arranged a football match, suggesting that participants should meet in the pubs before the game. Despite the presence of dragoons who had been brought over from Northampton, the 'players' soon got to work on the enclosure fences, and managed to tear them up and burn them.

The basis of the present rules and organization of soccer was established during the middle of last century. Until that time the public schools considered the game 'only fit for butcher boys'. But about 1850 it was seen that football could fit in with educational ideas. Football was to help encourage such qualities as 'group loyalty, willingness to compete according to rules, cooperativeness, courage, leadership ability, and the like'. Which is where schools got the idea of compulsory games.

What these schools did, together with some of the universities where their boys later moved, was to pave the way for football to become a nationwide game, by sorting out a single set of rules. This took many years to achieve, since those who adhered to the Harrow Rules, or the Eton Rules, or the Cambridge Rules did not always see the point of giving way to another school of thought.

Public nuisance?

Many reasons have been given over the centuries about why football should not be either played or watched. These are some typical reactions:

'In as much as there is great noise in the city caused by bustling over large balls ...from which many evils might arise which God forbid: we command and forbid on behalf of the king, on pain of imprisonment, such game to be used in the city in future.' Proclamation in London, 1314

'It is a custom which is disgraceful to humanity and civilization, subversive of good order and government, and destructive of the morals, properties, and very lives of our inhabitants.' Comments at the time of a player being killed in a game, 1796

'In the year 1847 the Derby football game was threatened with extinction. The mayor determined to suppress it as a public nuisance, conducive to riot and disorder.' Bygone Derbyshire, 1892

'Sport is very good in its way, but it must always hold a subordinate position. The end and aim of life is not sport, but to fill one's station in life in the most capable manner. It is well known to all that in factory, school and office the common everyday talk is sport, and the real business of life is neglected.' Letter to Birmingham Mail, 1908

'You play to win, and the play has little meaning unless you do your utmost to win. On the village green, where you pick up sides and no feeling of local patriotism is involved, it is possible to play simply for the fun and exercise, but as soon as the question of prestige arises, as soon as you feel that you and some large unit will be disgraced if you lose, the most savage combative instincts are aroused ... At the international level sport is frankly mimic warfare.' George Orwell, after the Moscow Dynamos' tour of Britain, 1945

The first action replay? A fourteenth-century tackle ready for viewing on a misericord in Gloucester Cathedral.

An early Italian version of the game.

This poem was written by a Benedictine monk at the beginning of the sixteenth century: evidently football was already keeping some people's minds off their work.

'The sturdy ploughman, lusty, strong, and bold,
Overcometh the winter with driving the football,
Forgetting labour and many a grievous fall.'

Only the goalkeeper to beat, with the defence left in a tangle in the shrubbery. Village football around 1800.

Into the towns

Many books dealing with the history of football imply that it was only the sons of the rich who kept the game going and then made it popular during this period. But football had not suddenly stopped outside the public schools and the universities during this period. The industrial revolution brought thousands from the country into the towns, and the game continued in the streets, though without the objections from Church and State to draw attention to its existence. With the restrictions on space involved in playing in the towns, such arts as dribbling began to assume more importance.

Probably the first important industrial centre for football was Sheffield, where at least two clubs were in existence by the time the Sheffield Rules were worked out in 1857; by 1862 there were fifteen. It was to the Sheffield Association that many of the new northern clubs affiliated, a short while after a small group of London-based clubs had formed the Football Association in 1863. The division between north and south affected the structure of football for a considerable period, causing rivalry between the FA and the Football League, between professionals and amateurs, between the industrial centres and the less urbanized regions.

The history of football is too often told in terms of the external landmarks in its development: the founding of the FA, how the Cup began, the founding of the League, the start of the World Cup competition, and so on. Though such things have their place, there is much more of interest to be found if the game is seen in relation to the social history of any given period. What did the average spectator look for from a visit to a football match? Why did the game become a professional one at the time it did? What sort of position did a player hold in society?

Really professional

To start with, why was the original League made up entirely of clubs from the north and the midlands? It seems that there were many reasons for this, not the least being the animosity that already existed between the south and the rest of the country, between the amateur gentlemen of leisure and the players in the industrial areas, who relied on the money that their clubs were already giving out. Payment for footballers very quickly became a hot issue, and only after years of bitter moralizing from those who could afford to play the game without reward, was the status of the professional player made legal in 1888. Scotland in particular proved especially puritanical over the issue of money, and since jobs were in short supply there, a large number of Scots players moved across the border, to seek a worthwhile club and a steady job.

Clubs then needed more money in order to pay their players' wages. The cup competition set up by the FA had by now drawn clubs from other parts of England. But if a club was knocked out in one of the early rounds, it was left with no more than friendly matches, and a few hastily arranged fixtures which drew in insufficient money.

On 2 March 1888 a small number of clubs employing professional players received a circular letter from William McGregor, a draper who had been closely involved with professional football in Birmingham. The letter said:

'. . .through cup-tie interferences, clubs are compelled to take on teams who will not attract the public. I beg to tender the following suggestion as a means of getting over the difficulty. That ten or twelve of the most prominent clubs in England combine to arrange fixtures each season, the said fixtures to be arranged at a friendly conference about the same time as the international conference. This combination might be known as the

The bicycle kick and the quick shouldering off the ball seem to have been around for at least a hundred years.

Association Football Union, and could be managed by a representative from each club. Of course this is in no way to interfere with the National Association, even the suggested matches might be played under cup-tie rules. . . . My object in writing to you at present is merely to draw your attention to the subject, and to suggest a friendly conference to discuss the matter more fully.'

At the 'friendly conference' the Football League was set up, and as there appeared to be only twenty-two Saturdays available during the season, the number of teams, despite many applications for membership, was confined to twelve, though as the regular fixtures proved popular, it very soon expanded in numbers.

Where were they then?
Individual clubs didn't just happen; they were created. The questions are why each one started where and when it did, why some have survived for decades while others have amalgamated or disappeared, and how certain towns and cities gradually became accustomed to football as part of their everyday life. If you live in Wolverhampton, for instance, you'll find that the 1974 League Cup winners started life as Goldthorn Football Club, and held their first meeting by permission of the vicar, in the local church school. A few weeks later the school's headmaster 'let the boys out earlier on Friday afternoon, and they had a Football Match'. The Wolves had started.

Schools or churches were very often the original force behind the formation of a club; equally often a group of working men put it together. West Ham, for example, began life as a professional club under the banner Thameside Ironworks, the name of a local shipbuilding yard in which the first players worked. After the Great War of 1914–18, football established itself as part of the community, and local businessmen began to get involved in the running of the club. Back in 1896, the MP for Fulham had noted that 'we have a football team before we have a town hall'. At that time he was probably complaining; by the 1920s he would have been boasting.

During the Depression many who were out of work or living in poverty saw football as the only relief from dole queues; the terraces were as much a part of the industrial landscape as the factory chimney, and were more often than not within shouting distance of it.

The value of a mass sport at a time of economic crisis has been seen in different ways. Is it a way of encouraging people to forget real cause for rebellion against bad living and working conditions, by providing another outlet for their emotions?

'Public sporting events provide a welcome opportunity to distract the masses politically and transform their applause for sporting achievements into acclamation for the political system.' Gerhard Vinnai, *Football Mania*

Or should it be seen as a symbol of defiance?

'Football was not so much an opiate of the people as a flag run up against the gaffer bolting his gates and the landlord armed with his bailiffs.' Arthur Hopcraft, *The Football Man*

Over 114 000 people turned up to the 1901 Cup Final. A contemporary report said: 'The conduct of these vast masses was, considering that it composed a football crowd, wonderfully good.'

Home and away

As individual players began to be noticed by large numbers of spectators, their fame spread outside their own communities. Yet their position remained a subordinate one. Financially they were very much subject to the whim of the businessmen who ran the clubs, particularly before the arrival of managers and coaches, who took the job of selecting the team out of their immediate hands. Plenty of profit was being made out of football, but the players appeared to be the last group to benefit. Certainly they remained very fixedly within the background from which they had come, although they were earning a little more than twice the average skilled worker's wage during the twenties and thirties. They were still largely looked upon as the local boys made good, the people's representatives who could still be found in the club or pub on a Saturday night.

It was not until after the Second World War, and in particular after the abolition of the maximum wage in 1961, that players were able to choose a style of life which would allow them to run a sports car, buy a five-bedroomed house in commuter country, and pay for their children's education. But even this style of life was only open to the highly paid few, and it's a matter for argument whether they became happier people by being wrenched out of the kind of communities in which they had been brought up.

Football and money

Football is a money spinner, whichever way you look at it. Star players, if not many others, get plenty of chances for perks as long as they remain at the top. Whether budding Johann Cruyffs will develop their skills more readily through buying Shredded Wheat is hardly the question: the Dutch striker is only one of many whose appearance at the breakfast table, on billboards and in TV commercials gives a generous boost to their bank balances. And publicity shots—such as Bobby Moore's imitation of the Pearly King a few days before the 1975 Cockney Cup Final—underline how the popularity of football has spread well beyond the sports pages of a newspaper.

Many commercial firms exploit consumer interest in the game by selling merchandise of one kind and another. The 1966 World Cup Finals in England provided a unique opportunity for exploiting the upsurge of interest in the national team, and souvenir sales brought in a cool £4 million. None was perhaps more successful than the World Cup Willie lion, a gimmick created by Walter Tuckwell who once worked for Walt Disney.

And then there's the pools. It's difficult to imagine life without the weekly flutter. The pools were started in the 1920s; they arose out of the small-scale gambling on the football results which people indulged in in pub, club or at the ground. By the 1950s it had become the seventh largest industry in Britain, providing work for around a hundred thousand people. Nowadays the pools companies turn over £200 000 million a year.

Getting your kicks early

'I would say that 90 per cent of the behaviour trouble we have in school football comes from the influence of television' Ken Aston, ex-referee and primary school head teacher

By the age of five, most kids have come across the game in some form or another. Their dad or mum might be regular supporters of the local club. In such cases, Saturday tea time is apt to be a more memorable meal than most others in the week, depending on how the home side has got on. Perhaps the kids in Alan Sillitoe's story *The Match* suffered more than most after the wrong side had won the game.

'He walked through the small living-room without speaking, took off his mac in the parlour. 'You should mek a fire in there,' he said, coming out. 'It smells musty. No wonder the clothes go to pieces inside six months.' His wife sat by the fire knitting from two balls of electric-blue wool in her lap. She was forty, the same age as Lennox, but gone to a plainness and discontented fat, while he had stayed thin and wiry for the same reason. Three children, the eldest a girl of fourteen, were at the table finishing tea.

Mrs Lennox went on knitting. 'I was going to make one today but I didn't have time.'

'Iris can mek one,' Lennox said, sitting down at the table.

The girl looked up. 'I haven't finished my tea yet, our dad.' The wheedling tone of her voice made him angry. 'Finish it later,' he said with a threatening look. 'The fire needs making now, so come on, look sharp and get some coal from the cellar.'

She didn't move, sat there with the obstinacy of the young spoiled by a mother. Lennox stood up. 'Don't let me have to tell you again.' Tears came into her eyes. 'Go on,' he shouted. 'Do as you're told.' He ignored his wife's plea to stop picking on her and lifted his hand to settle her with a blow.

'All right, I'm going. Look'—she got up and went to the cellar door. So he sat down again, his eyes roaming over the well-set table before him, holding his hands tightly clenched beneath the cloth. 'What's for tea then?' Alan Sillitoe, *The Loneliness of the Long Distance Runner*

Cup goal put boy on the road to recovery

A goal scored by Leeds United in the 1970 FA Cup Final put a road crash victim on to the road to recovery.

Martin Rohan, aged nine, had been unconscious for two months after the accident. When he revived he could not recognise his parents. But as his father sat with him at his hospital bedside watching on TV his team, Leeds, struggle against Chelsea, centre forward Mick Jones scored a second goal.

For the first time since the crash Martin—a fervent Leeds supporter—"came back to life." He smiled.

"After that he seemed to get better quickly," said his mother, Margaret. "I went to see him next day, and he recognised me. Doctors had only given him 12 hours to live after the crash. I never thought he would ever get better. That goal obviously played a part."

If nobody in the family watches football it's more than likely that part of a game, or at the very least the football results, will have been seen on television. Or the kids will have come across other children knocking a ball around a street or the nearest patch of grass.

In and out of school. Will the future bring 'O' levels in football?
Or is it more exciting as an escape from school—catching a glimpse of the Brazilian team in training for the 1974 World Cup.

Players at school

Even before school begins, football provides a chance for young kids to form and test friendships, to get used to conflict, to experience praise as well as criticism from others of their age. It's a game where skills are picked up without being taught, at a pace and in an order which the child decides for himself. So much of school life is directed by teachers, with the emphasis either on good behaviour or solid learning: playground football provides an activity without ability groups, where no formal demands for progress are being made.

Ultimately football becomes a 'subject', and makes its appearance on the timetable under the heading of 'games'. Enter the adult, not always welcomed happily by the young players. Here is Billy Casper's games teacher in *Kestrel for a Knave* (filmed as *Kes*).

'The team broke for their appropriate halves, and while they were arguing their claims for positions, Mr Sugden jogged to the sideline, dropped the ball, and took off his tracksuit. Underneath he was wearing a crisp red football shirt with white cuffs and a white band round the neck. A big white 9 filled most of the back, whiter than his white nylon shorts, which showed a slight fleshy tint through the material. He pulled his socks up, straightened the ribs, then took a fresh roll of half-inch bandage from his tracksuit and ripped off two lengths. The torn bandage packet, the cup of its structure still intact, blew away over the turf like the damaged shell of a dark blue egg. Mr Sugden used the length of bandage to secure his stockings just below the knees, then he folded his tracksuit neatly on the ground, looked down at himself, and walked on to the pitch carrying the ball like a plum pudding on the tray of his hand. Tibbut, standing on the centre circle, with his hands down his shorts, winked at his left winger and waited for Mr Sugden to approach.

'Who are you today, sir, Liverpool?'

'Rubbish, lad! Don't you know your club colours yet?'

'Liverpool are red, aren't they, sir?'

'Yes, but they're all red, shirts, shorts and stockings. These are Manchester United's colours.'

'Course they are, sir, I forgot. What position are you playing?'

Mr Sugden turned his back on him to to show him his number 9.

'Bobby Charlton. I thought you were usually Denis Law when you were Manchester United.'

'It's too cold to play as a striker today. I'm scheming this morning, all over the field like Charlton.'

'Law plays all over, sir. He's not only a striker.'

'He doesn't link like Charlton.'

'Better player though, sir.'

Sugden shook his head. 'No, he's been badly off form recently.'

'Makes no odds, he's still a better player. He can settle a game in two minutes.'

'Are you trying to tell *me* about football, Tibbut?'

'No, sir.'

'Well shut up then. Anyway Law's in the wash this week.' Barry Hines, *Kestrel for a Knave*

Billy himself hated football, never had his kit, was always being forced to keep goal, and was for ever being got at by Mr Sugden. So what about all those others like him, who find themselves out in the cold when school teams start being selected

A former inspector of physical education in London has recently suggested that competitive games like football should only play a small part in the ordinary school day, since more children were branded as failures than successes as a result of team selections. His solution was for schools to

---

The dirty mucky 'oller

O me lads, wasn't it the gear
Those footee matches that we
    played
That seemed to last a year.
Ev'ry day of the holidays
Ar kid I would foller
To have a game of footee
In the dirty mucky 'oller.

There must have been a hundred
    of us
Itchin' for a kick
So me and Tommy Riley the sides
    we quickly picked
There was a little mix-up, no-one
    wanted Billy Tracey
But we had to have him in ar side
Because he owned the casey.

We kicked-off after breakfast and
We played til eight at night
With scores like 80–63 it really was
    a sight;
We was trailing 50–41 when they
    all went for their dinner
And I was left there on me tod
And slyly scored the winner.

Words: Bob Alker   Tune: Blaydon Races

develop a gymnastic programme, which would allow children to develop their individual abilities rather than have them held up against those of their classmates. Another criticism of the way football is organized in schools comes from a head teacher in Lancashire, who has suggested that school league competitions should be banned. His view is that children don't need cups and competitions to get fun out of a sport, and that these kind of competitions bring out the worst in everyone. 'What has league football got to do with education?' he asks. 'If the slate were wiped clean and we started again, would we allow school sport to develop in the way it has?'

Of course it's very often the case that the kids who fail at academic subjects are the best performers on the playing fields. Some become fanatical enough about one particular game for them to lose interest in nearly all the rest of school life. Barry Hines, the author of *Kes*, clearly belonged to this group.

'I went to a grammar school, but I was completely unacademic. I could never raise any enthusiasm for Palmerston's foreign policy, or the rainfall on the pampas. The only rainfall I was bothered about was the one outside the classroom window that might prevent us from going out for games.

If the weather was too bad—for the teachers, never for us— and we couldn't have games, it was a major disaster; the week was spoiled. If we had to play any other game but football—the PE master used to go off his head occasionally and make us play rugby and shinty—I used to go into a murderous sulk and refuse to lower myself. I was always glad I wasn't a clever boy in the A form. I used to feel sorry for them, they had fewer games lessons than the rest of us.'

Perhaps we should question whether games should be on the timetable at all or at least why it can't be made an optional activity. Why are football and other sports generally considered 'a good thing', even for those who hate joining in? Is it still a question of building character, of the battle of life being won inside the penalty area? 'Sport develops moderation, restraint, control of the emotions and other manly virtues,' wrote a leading sports critic in

In *Stubby* (a Swedish film directed by Bo Wideberg), a six-year-old boy is called into the Swedish team after beating the national hero in a playground kickabout. Though he's too young to tie his own bootlaces or read about his performance in the papers, Stubby helps the team to reach the World Cup Finals. Eventually he gets fed up with all the pressures of a footballer's job, and goes back to an ordinary home and school life.

1896, and many educational thinkers and teachers over the last eighty years or so have echoed his view.

A more original opinion was put forward a few years later by the famous psycho-analyst Sigmund Freud, who declared:

'Modern education, as we know, makes great use of games in order to divert young people from sexual activity.'

Has the plan worked then?

Maybe Barry Hines would have had a better time in school if an idea of Matt Busby's had been taken up. The former manager of Manchester United suggested in his autobiography that there should be a GCE exam in football, that if you have football ability you should be allowed to qualify in it. Not such a crazy idea when you come to think of it—but would such an exam simply be testing ball skills, or would you have to answer questions on paper like 'Account for the relegation of Carlisle to Division Two in 1975, with reference to the industry and geographical position of the town'?

Those who can, play; those who can't, read about it

Plenty of kids are lousy at playing football, but are no less keen on following the game; through the magazines, on television, or by going along with one of their parents or brothers and sisters or friends to the local ground. How is football put over to young readers through the magazines, comics and annuals that come out throughout the year?

Some of the long-running comics, such as the *Wizard* and *Hotspur*, still print football serials in the tradition of the pre-war 'Roy of the Rovers', though nowadays they often have an element of science fiction in them. Here's the plot summary at the start of a recent episode in *Hotspur*'s 'The Lost Team from Eterna':

'For twenty years after a plane crash, the players of Sandford City were held prisoner in a lost city in the South American jungle. Forced to play football to entertain their captors, they were kept young by the mysterious powers of a strange idol. At last they escaped, taking the idol with them but pursued by the Guardian, the High Priest of the idol. Returning home they successfully took over struggling Sandford United. Away to Midhampton City in a cup-tie, the new United were one goal down but team captain Jeff Kane was leading the fight back.'

Whether this sort of stuff will appeal to a committed young football fan is doubtful. To be fair, the comic as a whole is aimed at a very general young readership, so it's no surprise to find a rather limp plot mixed in with the fortunes of Sandford City.

Suicide by fan as team flopped

A Sheffield Wednesday supporter, depressed at the performance of his team, which was last season relegated to the Third Division for the first time in its 109-year history, committed suicide with a large overdose of drugs, an inquest at Sheffield heard yesterday.

This seventeen year old fan took his interest too seriously.

It's really the annuals and the magazines such as *Goal*, *Shoot* and *Soccer* which demonstrate what the publishing companies think will sell to kids. In 1974 *Goal* was incorporated into *Shoot*, after the first appearance of *Soccer*, 'The Great New Football Monthly for Boys'. A survey was made which looked into the reading habits of boys and girls over 10, and it was found that about 16 per cent of the boys aged 12 or more were reading *Shoot*.

The magazine's editor feels that it is 'the pace-setter in the world of football magazines'. His judgment seems to be that the readers will be happy with an abundance of action photos, questions of the 'Who was Gillingham's top scorer last season' variety, and a clutch of articles written for some of the top players by football journalists.

Soccer at first glance seems to have a more varied and imaginative selection of material, finding space for articles on the right of TV commentators to make judgments on controversial incidents, on how boys become professional footballers, on the problem of violent play for both the referee and the players, and so on. It manages to provide something other than the stream of action, goals, sensations and worship that characterize its rivals.

But *Soccer* runs what it calls 'soccer strip action'. If you look at one of the early issues you find that almost half of the space is devoted to a story in comic strip form called 'The Hard Man'. The plot concerns a slightly built but talented young player called Terry Naylor, who is told by all around him that he's not strong enough to make the grade. The story is interesting for the message that it puts over. It's made clear that hardness off the field is a manly quality, and that a similar attitude on the field will be its own reward. Below are a few frames which show how, in just a year, Terry changed from a weakling to the 'hard man' of the team.

In annuals there are some longer, more thoughtful pieces, where the assumption is that kids are interested in other things than statistics and the sayings of the stars. But no one has yet put out a magazine which catches the excitement of football, and yet treats the players as human beings, not gods. Perhaps it can't be done, and football mags only sell if the game is given the glamour treatment.

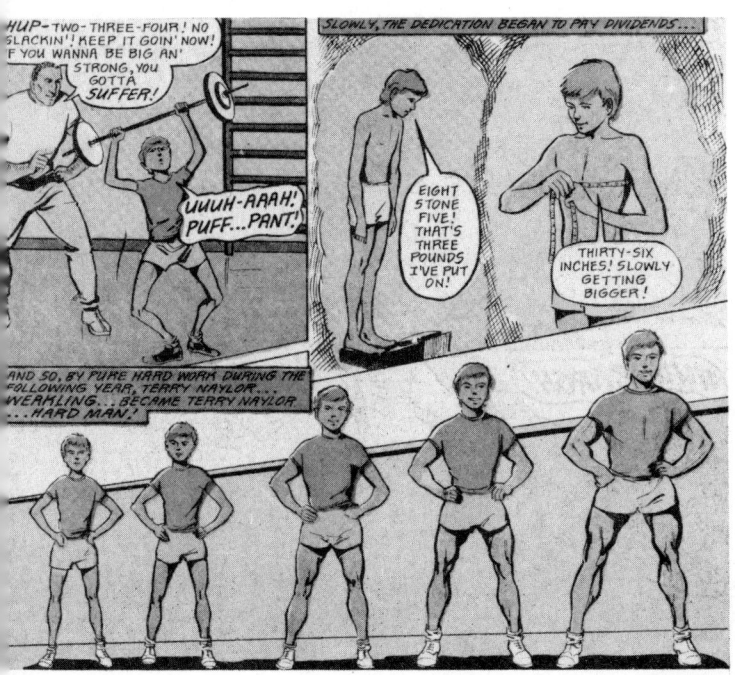

Don't shoot the goalkeeper...

The greatest save?
'...towards the blurred object now hurtled Pelé, leaping over Mullery and heading the ball down towards a layer of black netting, and all for one were shouting goal and rising to acclaim the 'King'. What happened next remained indistinct in the memory, a blurred and outrageous flash of movement, a combination of sprawling arms and legs. Banks was suddenly over to the right of goal lying sideways with his left leg thrust out straight, his right leg bent at right angles and his groping right hand scooping the ball up and over the crossbar. What he had in fact done, was to reach a ball going at outrageous speed at a point when most other goalkeepers would have not even moved.... It was surely the save of the twentieth century. Already it has become a legend in the game, a piece of unique folklore, a gymnastic impossibility.' John Moynihan, *Football Fever*

The last save
John Thomson was nicknamed 'The Prince of Goalkeepers', for his supreme agility and astonishing reflexes in the Celtic goal. He became Scotland's goalkeeper at the age of twenty-two, but a year later in 1931 was killed after diving at the feet of the Rangers centre forward. Thirty thousand people turned out to his funeral; at his memorial service in Glasgow the theme of the sermon was 'Greater love hath no man than this, that he lay down his life for his friends'.

Gordon Banks punches clear from Alan Gilzean.

John Thomson's last save. His ghost is believed to haunt the Celtic net.

...he's only doing his best

Go to the back

'The goals were about twenty yards wide; the ball, to score a goal, had to pass at any height between two trees at either end, and had to hit the rails or pass over them. The small boys, the duffers, and the funk-sticks were the goalkeepers, twelve or fifteen at each end, and were spread out across this wide space; if any fellow who was playing out showed any sign of 'funk', or failed to play up, he was packed off into goal at once, not only for that day, but as a lasting degradation. On the other hand, if any goalkeeper made a good save of a goal, he was called for immediately to play out, and thenceforth he played out always.' H. C. Benham, 'Football at Westminster School'

One's company

'By the very nature of his art and duties, the goalkeeper is inclined to be an explosive and temperamental fellow who needs his stage if he is to function properly. This stage is increasingly cluttered with the boots and bodies of his fellow defenders; a situation which is growing worse rather than better.... What we see before us, a manifest sign of the times, is the transformation of the goalkeeper from flamboyant individualist into a grey company man.' Brian Glanville

Holland's first goal in the 1974 World Cup, against Uruguay.

Strong support from the back from goalkeeper Ray Clemence.

Sit down, you hooligans

'The foundations of discipline are not being laid in the school.' Secretary of Manchester United Football Club
'A society that makes its lustiest members clerks and messenger boys should not be surprised when they lash back in the easiest way possible.' Chris Lightbown in *Foul* magazine

A few years ago, if you were young, rode a motorbike and made a noise in cafés, you were marked down as one of this particular species. Today you still have to be young, but now your flock has migrated to football grounds. You are:

'Not supporters really'—Secretary, Federation of Supporters Clubs

'loutish scum'—national football journalist

'disgracing the name of the British people'—Chairman of Spurs.

You have been the subject of an official report by a group of Birmingham bird watchers, and you are given more column inches in the press than the sayings of Enoch Powell. You are no longer a rare bird, but many people would prefer you to be extinct. You are a 'hooligan'.

Ladder line-up to protect windows, and a pre-match police line-up.

Who rules?

'I don't know what the answer is,' said a Cardiff headmaster. The question is: what is the question? To begin with, have you noticed that almost all discussions about young people and football very quickly turn to the question of violence, on or off the terraces? The argument is usually conducted in terms of disrespect for authority, damage to property, or the supposed subnormality of the kids involved.

Well, who decides on these themes? Is it the newspapers and the television companies, from whom we have to get so much of our information? If so, where do they get their material from? They are frequently quoting 'a spokesman of' the Football League, the club, the police, the courts, almost all of whom are over forty. But how often do they call upon a spokesman from the Stretford End or the Shed, to at least, provide the famous 'balance' that journalists and television interviewers and presenters are supposed to be aiming for? Perhaps they wouldn't find comments from such a source acceptable—particularly if this supporter's view of football were thought to be at all typical:

'Football is about hitching, getting pissed, shouting, standing, pushing, pissing on your boots or the guy in front's legs, singing, chanting, surging and swaying, scarves, and if you feel like it, AGGRO!'

There used to be a very popular theory which stated that it was viciousness on the field by the professionals that sparked off the same thing behind the goals. Not too many people seem to be convinced by this argument these days. For one thing, why is the label 'hooligan' never applied to a Rugby supporter, even when he witnesses a player's ear being bitten off? And then, why do off-the-field incidents that make the front pages of newspapers almost always occur at games which are not especially violent?

Increasingly, people are looking outside the game for the causes of aggressive behaviour before, during and after matches. A 1968 Government Report *Soccer Hooliganism*, which borrowed its title from a newspaper headline, looked at the occupations of nearly 500 people convicted for offences at soccer matches.

School or apprentice	79
Unskilled/labourer	206
Semi-skilled	112
Skilled	50
Salesman/clerical	19
Professional/managerial	2
Not known or unemployed	29
Total	497

These figures give us some idea of how those who get into trouble with police *inside* the ground spend the rest of their week: mostly in jobs in which routine, boredom and frustration play a large part. Coming more up to date and back to the younger supporters, a high proportion of those arrested during the 1973–4 season were in the 13–17 age group. But you don't need either of these sets of figures to work out that the young who are turned on by football are more often than not, those turned off their work or their school.

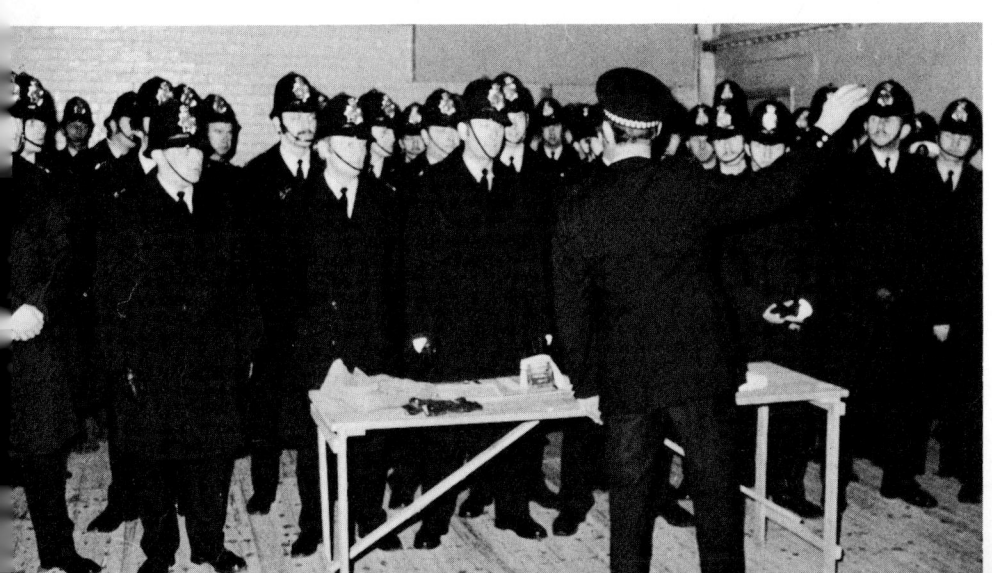

'We don't have to stick rigidly to the itinerary lad. Constable says we can report to the station first if we like.'

Rival fans at the Cardiff v Manchester United match menace each other behind barriers and police.

Test your hooliganism

Everyone has their own ideas about the attractions of football. If you go regularly, or just now and then, or have a friend or two who does, try this test out on them. Marks for agreeing with certain statements are in brackets after each one, but you're allowed to give higher or lower if you want. Alternatively, tear this lot up and make your own list; then put the completed test in an envelope and send it to the secretary of your nearest league club.

You're only allowed to choose three of these statements (points in brackets). If you score 0–5 you'll never make it as a hooligan: you might as well sit in the stand. If you score 6–12 you'll probably need a couple of season's regular practice before you can achieve your first detention order. If you score 13–20 you should be up to making your first unaccompanied sortie behind the enemy goal. If you score 21–24 you'll be known to every British Rail stationmaster in the land, you'll be asked to appear in a television documentary about the generation gap, and your mates will offer to hold your scarf aloft for you while you lead the next chant.

I go to football because:

Everyone else will be there (5)
I want to watch the game (0)
There's nothing else to do (4)
I might get my left arm on Match of the Day (2)
Anything is better than going to work/school (6)
I hate Nottingham Forest (or whoever the visitors are) (8)
I collect the programmes (1)
I enjoy the community singing (3)
I want to get at the enemy's supporters (9)
I dislike policemen (7)

The other timetable

After all, what is a school? All too often it is a place where an older generation tell the young what to do, how to do it, and even what to wear while they're doing it. As these two East End kids found out after a meeting with their head teacher:

'She saw me and Bob in the corridor and that we was in our skinhead uniform and she said, 'March after me up to my room.' And then we was marching after 'er and she told us to pick up a bit of paper and I told 'er I worn't no dustman. Then she told us to go 'ome and take off our uniform and not to come back until we did...so we went 'ome and never come back to school again.' *The Paint House: Words from an East End Gang*

On the terraces you can organize your own timetable: assembly, musical appreciation, English language, RE, physical activity. All are there, though not quite in the style any teacher might have hoped for. Your uniform is optional, but it is fixed by your group, and not by the school outfitter.

Peter Terson wrote a play called *Zigger Zagger*, about the life of a group of football fans. At their last school assembly they turned the hymn into a surging chant for 'City'. The head teacher was not amused:

'I see as usual our effort was spoilt by the vociferous minority. The gang who only feel something when they have a red and white scarf round their necks. The people who are only brave in a 50 000 crowd. The people who have got nothing out of school life, and put nothing in. The people who think all the world's a football pitch. For the rest of us there are more things in life than football.'

Well, it probably depends on what those other things are. For all those hundreds of kids who leave school every year to go straight into a dead-end job, there is a tremendous feeling of being kicked to the bottom of the heap. An afternoon behind the goal with your mates is still one of the best and cheapest ways of briefly coming alive again. And of course you are seen by others, and that doesn't just mean the television cameras. Certainly during the build-up to the kick-off, groups on the terraces like the Kop at Liverpool or the Chelsea Shed are the focus of attention, providing most of the noise and the colour. If you're part of the group you feel yourself at the centre of the stage; you know that some of the other spectators have come as much to watch the spectacle you lay on before and during the match as they have to watch the game itself.

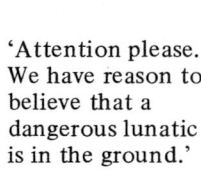

'Attention please. We have reason to believe that a dangerous lunatic is in the ground.'

Sacred turf

Not that the clubs welcome any help in arranging the show. There are some moves afoot to restrict the movements of young supporters. Ideas for moats, fences, pens, identity cards are all being considered seriously, while one or two clubs already spend around £10 000 a year to hire closed-circuit TV, pay marshals from the supporters clubs, and employ 'spotters' with long-range glasses and radio. It has even been suggested that the terraces should be left empty!

Of course some of these ideas are designed to keep kids off the pitch rather than off each other. But invading the sacred turf, which has caused such alarm amongst club officials and directors, is not a new phenomenon. There was the game at Hampden Park in 1886 between Preston North End and Queen's Park, when the home team's centre-forward was the victim of a violent tackle from behind, five minutes before the end.

'Then the game was finished. The indignant crowd now surged onto the field, maddened with passion, shouting, waving sticks, umbrellas, and such like weapons, and the North End team were at once engulfed in a living sea, which rolled round them in angry surging waves that threatened to engulf them at any moment.'

In this case there seems to have been a

Circled—three helmetless policemen in the rioting crowd at White Hart Lane. PC Carrington is on the right.

spontaneous burst of collective anger which spilled out on to the pitch. But modern invasions are sometimes more calculated, though who is to say whether acute disappointment or careful planning was most responsible for the invasion of the pitch at Old Trafford when Manchester United were finally relegated in the summer of 1974.

But why weren't fences erected at Hampden all those years ago? Was it something to do with the age of the invaders? So what are kids looking for nowadays when they jump the railings? Is it just follow my leader; a need to be noticed; or a desire to play at least a minor part in the afternoon's entertainment? Seven years after he wrote *Zigger Zagger* Peter Terson saw it like this:

'Perhaps it's a subconscious desire to take the centre of the stage. It would be interesting if you said to a fan club, all right, you give a display. Now, Ladies and Gentlemen, the Manchester United Fan Club will build the biggest human pyramid ever seen. Perhaps that's what's needed: a ritual in which *they* take the pitch.'

State of the game.

Look out Division One—United fans smash another ground

X-CERTIFICATE!

These thugs are showing in your town next season

DO you want Manchester United in your town? With one of the finest club sides of the past 20 years go just about the biggest set of thugs in the country! Sadly you can't have one without the other.

Win or lose, a section of fans smear the name of United and Soccer leaving a trail of destruction in cities throughout Britain. They're arrogant in victory and nasty in defeat.

THE SOUVENIR HUNTERS—Manchester United fans race on the rampage across the Notts County pitch with the remains of a crash-barrier—a "prize" of their team's title triumph

Railmen call strike on day of big match

LONDON Tube train staff are threatening a 24-hour walkout in protest at soccer hooliganism.

They aim to stop Tube services on May 24—the day of the next England-Scotland match at Wembley.

And they are asking for support from busmen, as well as from other railwaymen.

FAN BAN

FAN BEATEN UP BY A COP

A MAN thrown out of a football ground by a policeman had a broken spine, broken nose and a black eye, a court heard yesterday.

Ipswich supporter Brian Jacobs was taken to hospital by spectators.

The man who ejected him, PC Brian Shuttleworth, appeared at Shrewsbury Crown Court accused of assault.

Granny offside in soccer punch-up

After a noisy incident when Stourbridge had played Weymouth at home in the period of Christmas goodwill — an incident in which a footballer got punched in the mouth and a linesman was struck with a rattle on a 2ft pole— Mrs Alice Dakin has been banned from attending any more matches at the Stourbridge ground. She is 60, and a grandmother.

Jail the thugs call

SPORTS MINISTER Denis Howell will be told today: "Crack down on Soccer hooligans—send them to prison."

Keeping in touch

There's more emotion spent these days on the subject of pitch invasions than on almost any other topic in football. But the relationship between the crowd and the players has always been at the heart of football's popularity. One historian has suggested that the spectators of the 1920s and 1930s, when professional football was well established as a national sport, had no need to jump the barriers: they could still feel that the club belonged to them, so there was no need for the ritual 'capture' of the playing area that is so popular today.

With all the transfers that take place, today's top players have no strong connections with the area in which their club is situated, and are much more cut off from the everyday life of their supporters. But supporters are still caught up in a strong web of feeling, both toward individuals and teams.

The excessive exposure and attention given to football personalities by the media tends to overglamourize them. Players are the objects of anger, frustration, love, admiration, and it's not surprising that some of these spill over on to the pitch. Though players consistently come in for abuse and scorn, they also feed off the support of their followers. 'You can feel the warmth coming off the Kop,' says Kevin Keegan, who plays for a highly successful team in front of the most ardent supporters in England.

Top: February 1926. Clapton Orient v Newcastle United in the FA Cup. Wood, Orient's captain, is greeted by fans.
Bottom: October 1972. Italian soccer fans chase the victorious rival team off the field.

Top: the 1932 Cup Final. Newcastle's captain Nelson carries the Cup away while fans clap him on the back.
Bottom: the latest precaution at Old Trafford, Manchester United's ground. No touching the players here.

More in sorrow than in anger: a Leeds supporter after the Final.

The bill for damage after Leeds had lost the 1975 European Cup to Bayern Munich was £20 000. Were the fans or the Paris police the main culprits? Leeds had their two-year ban from Europe cut to one after they had provided the authorities with 'additional information' on the incidents.

From the terrace

Participation being the fashionable idea, if not practice, of this decade, a few clubs have made some token gestures towards their supporters, such as letting them on the pitch on a Sunday to 'meet' the players. Bill Leivers, the manager at Cambridge, went one further, with the idea of opening football clubs up to their young supporters and potential players. Leivers had outlined a scheme for meetings, at both the ground and at schools, between players and schoolboys, where there would be a chance to talk at length to the players, the manager, and others involved in running the club. However, before he could get the scheme started Leivers was given the push as a result of Cambridge's disappointing results during the previous eighteen months.

But will *any* of these suggestions and schemes make any difference to the way a young supporter feels about his own team? Should clubs perhaps accept that conflict is all part of the attraction, and carry on with their policy of keeping the customers dissatisfied?

'The steps are as greasy as a school playground lavatory in the rain. The air is rancid with beer and onions and belching and worse. The language is a gross purple of obscenity. When the crowd surges at a shot or a collision near the corner flag a man or a boy, and sometimes a girl, can be lifted off the ground in the crush as if by some massive, soft-sided crane grab and dangled about for minutes on end, perhaps never getting back to within four or five steps of the spot from which the monster made its bite. In this incomparable entanglement of bodies and emotions lies the heart of the fan's commitment to football.'
Arthur Hopcraft, *The Football Man*

In this part of *Football Man*, Arthur Hopcraft was remembering the terraces he stood on in his youth; what he calls 'Those privileged places of working-class communion'. Now it seems that the days of worship may be coming to an end, as some of the richer clubs are converting much of their standing space into seats, in the name of the great god, 'Family Entertainment.' One angry supporter took a look into the future:

'Their Utopia is a spotless concrete bowl lined with thousands of little blue plastic seats, lots of clean toilets, a restaurant, a sports complex, piped muzak, and 22 clean-cut goal-hungry young zombies playing the game in a spirit of friendship and sportsmanship on a plasti-grass pitch. They want matches which end in 7–7 draws, watched by packed crowds of middle-class parents who have each brought their 2.4 children, who cheer enthusiastically every goal, applaud every exhibition of skill from the opposition, and who go home afterwards in their family saloons, all agreeing that they have been thoroughly entertained.' Letter to *Foul* magazine

A chilling fantasy—or the shape of things to come? Clearly only a small number of well-off clubs will be able to afford much improvement in their facilities during the next few years. They are already petrified by falling attendances and blood-red bank balances, so can they risk losing their noisiest but often most loyal supporters?

Football poem — Roger McGough

Im an ordinary feller 6 days of the week
But satday I turn into a football freak.
Im a schizofanatic, sad burrits true
One half of me's red, and the other half's blue.

I cant make me mind up which team to support
Whether to lean to starboard or port
Id be bisexual if I had time for sex
Cos its Goodison one week and Anfield the next.

And the worse time of all is Derby day
One half of me's at home and the other's away
But I get down there early all ready for battle
With me rainbow scarf and me two-tone rattle.

And Im shoutin for Latchford and Im shoutin for Hughes
'Come on de Poole' — 'Gerrin dere Blues'
'Give it ter Keegan' — 'What a puddin'
'King of der Kop' — All of a sudden — Wop!
'Goal!' — 'Offside!'

And after the match as I walk back alone
Its argue, argue all the way home
Somenights when Im drunk Ive even let fly
An give meself a poke in the eye.

But in front of the fire watchin Match of the Day
Tired but happy, I look arn't this way:
Part of me's lost and part of me's won
Ive had twice the heartaches—but Ive had twice the fun.

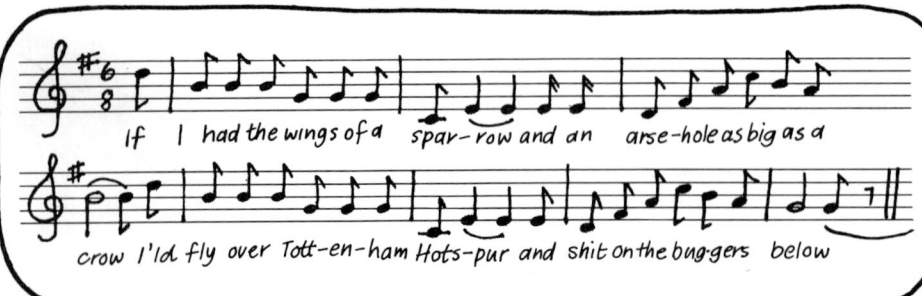

Football kisses
Tom Pickard

It's in the net
Not quite pet
Hero, pudding
You stupid git
Wat a good'un
It's off his heel
It's in, it's not
He lacks speed
What a farce
Next time, use your arse
It slipped off his boot like
A greased rat off a bent pike
Hero, gutter snipe
Cream of the scum
With a heel like that you should be hung
Lovers, lovers, football brothers
Rejects, dejects, clowns and crackers
Boot'em one in the knackers
He's on the floor, not anymore
Get it back, give him a crack
Lob it, stop it, put the block on it
Watch your teeth, his elbow's lethal
He's trying, he's tripped, he's flying
Did you see a chip?
I'll buy him
Lovers, lovers, football brothers
Rejects, dejects, clowns and crackers
Boot 'em one in the knackers.

You'll never walk alone

Certainly the Football League officials seem keen to make the grounds fit places for our aunties to come to. Not so long ago they tried to get all the swear words cut out of the singing and chanting which comes from behind the goals. Their idea was to organize a competition for choirs from different grounds, with the chance of 'a holiday in an exotic European resort' for the winners. Said a spokesman:

'They can sing what they like, but we are not having filth. They could use original songs or put their own words to well-known ones. Some crowds are very witty, we know, but we want to clean up the yobbo sections, who aren't really concerned with what happens in the game.'

One generation trying to dictate terms to another again: but did the League *really* expect to be taken seriously? Their statement is more interesting for the polite reference to 'yobbos' in the final sentence. Note how the word is used to describe anyone who might join in the chorus of 'Nice One, Cyril'—or worse. Again and again, the people in authority inside football claim that trouble and disturbance only come from a tiny group of hardened delinquents who have no interest in the game. But as Michael Parkinson has put it:

'Unless the yobbos have employed the augmented talents of the Huddersfield Choral Society and the Red Army Choir to help them out (which is unlikely for various reasons), they are a very large and loud minority indeed.'

It should be clear to most supporters that loyalty and aggression can go together, and even the authors of *Soccer Hooliganism* had to admit:

'We have been impressed by the amount of knowledge and memory for detail possessed by fans of limited intelligence and intellectual background.'

Perhaps such people have never experienced the excitement and the fear of being part of a frenzied crowd. You don't have to be a teenager or be unemployed to find yourself swept along, as this teacher's experience at Wembley in 1974 shows.

'It was the first time that England had played Argentina since the famous game in the 1966 World Cup, after which Alf Ramsey had described the South Americans as "animals". This time only Argentina were through to the Finals, due to be played at Munich in three weeks' time. Ramsey had just been fired, but we remembered his words as the South Americans began chopping down the English players. "Eng-land! Eng-land!" gave way to "An-i-mals! An-i-mals!" England hit back, with skill and two goals. In the last twenty minutes Argentina turned on the style that was always in them, and pulled level with a penalty. We were above the tunnel as the players hobbled in at the whistle. The chanting rose again, sometimes "Eng-land!", sometimes "An-i-mals!" My friend and I screamed with the rest of them. I picked up a beer can and hurled it at a striped shirt going into the tunnel. It only hit the whitewashed wall. We turned away, and two middle-aged, responsible members of society struck for home, angry and frustrated.'

Just sign here, lad...

> 'I tell any father that asks me that only one lad in ten thousand will make it.'
> Bill Elliott, Newham Schools FA under-16s manager

> **'They've mixed with world-class players. They might not measure up to our standards, because we demand the highest, but they can always go elsewhere.'**
> Pat Welton, Spurs youth team manager

When is an apprentice not an apprentice?

As many young players know to their cost, the Football League run something called an apprentice scheme. Now an apprentice is normally defined as a person who receives instruction in the skills of a trade, in exchange for a promise of several years employment with his master. During that period the apprentice is tutored carefully in the necessary skills while receiving a weekly wage which will keep him alive, but which will be low in relation to what he can expect to earn when he has served his apprenticeship. Professional football seems to depart from this practice as follows:

1. An apprentice will often receive only minimal coaching and training, being used as a foil for the full-time professionals.
2. An apprentice will certainly receive a low wage, but he can not be certain of moving on to a good wage when the apprentice period runs out.
3. An apprentice will be extremely fortunate if he is allowed to exercise his skills professionally, and doubly so if able to do so for a League club, even a Fourth Division one.
4. An apprentice will normally only be contracted to a club for two years. If he cancels his registration or refuses the professional contract offered him, he cannot play for another club for two years.

This scheme, and the connected associate schoolboy one which precedes it, gives an insight into some of the attitudes to young players which are held by those running the game. There are some clubs who do a lot for their boys, but the variation in facilities, opportunity and honesty mean that a large number every year suffer acute disappointment when they fail to make the grade. As one boy who failed described it:

'Apart from sparse training I spent most of the time as a skivvy round the club. First I was the toilet cleaner—as well as other cleaning tasks—and later I had one of the best jobs of all. I became bootboy, from the age of seventeen until I was eighteen and a half.... Suddenly I was told that I was too old to be an apprentice pro. I was completely heartbroken. It was just like the end of the world to me. I felt I had been used as cheap labour all those years when I thought I was doing quite well and would make the first team.'

Letting them know

But it's not just the scheme itself that is so unfair; it is also the way it is used and presented by some of the clubs. To a young player who may be the star not only of his school team but perhaps also of the county team, a possible career as a professional will naturally have a great deal of appeal. Unfortunately it is in the interests of people involved with the club to play on the schoolboy's idea of a player's life, an idea which he will have built up as a result of the treatment given to players by the media.

So there is always a conflict. The clubs will not admit responsibility for causing damage to the lives of many young people, the majority of whom will be shown the stadium gates at the age of eighteen. 'We encourage our boys to attend the local technical college' is the standard answer to the charge that the drop-outs have been left behind while others have obtained qualifications. But boys will not be inclined to study business management or salesmanship as long as they think that others are devoting that time to improving their chances of making the first team.

CONTACT between beginners and the senior players is natural at Arsenal ... the football club where it's always 'all for one, one for all.'

Top: part of a publicity booklet which 'describes the challenges and the rewards which await the boys who make their dream of being part of Arsenal'.
Bottom: joking apart, apprentices have plenty of menial jobs to do, as even George Best found before he made the first team (right).

A losing game

Clubs do provide approved hostels or digs for apprentices, but not even a marble palace will conceal the fact that most of its residents are on to a losing game. Many of the new apprentices will have been taken away from their familiar home environment for the first time. For example, the very day I was up at Arsenal meeting their chief scout, he had been talking to Harry Griffith about joining the club. But Swansea City's young midfield player had felt homesick for Wales and returned to his home, after being on loan to Arsenal for exactly two days.

The apprentices are thrown amongst people who demand a high degree both of physical fitness and social conformity. Alec Stock, an experienced manager, expresses a typical view. 'A boy who lets his hair grow below his collar-line, or wears jeans or an outlandishly cut jacket, will soon be put in his place. This is primarily a team game; the boy who wants to be an individual in the way he dresses, soon wants to be an individual on the field.'

Why should this be so? If Alan Taylor or Brian Little had gone around in tatty jeans with dirt behind their ears, would this have affected their heading ability in front of goal? Little wonder that many of the young players can't stand the pace, and actually leave of their own accord.

Clubs will say that the reasons for the rejects not making the grade lie within the young player himself. They talk about lack of application, failure to fulfil early promise, lack of physical development or homesickness, but miss out the fact that the system as presently organized means that there will *have* to be many more failures than successes.

Changes, changes

Will this system remain? Well, some things are changing. Now that the school-leaving age has been raised to sixteen, there is only a year instead of two between the time when a boy leaves school and the earliest moment he can turn professional. The Education Officer for the players' union, Bob Kerry, thinks the system is an iniquitous one, but that boys may find it easier to wait until they are seventeen and eligible for a professional contract, instead of becoming an apprentice for one year only.

A further hopeful sign comes from the fact that players such as Duncan McKenzie and David Cross (A Levels) and Brian Hall, Steve Heighway and Alan Gowling

The lucky few

At the beginning of the 1974/75 season I carried out my own little bit of research, since it seemed very difficult to get a clear idea of what life as an apprentice might be like for anyone seriously interested in trying to join a League club. I sent a questionnaire to the 44 first and second division clubs, asking them for information about conditions, facilities, wages and opportunities for young players up to the age of 18, so that their answers could be included in this book. Less than a quarter of them bothered to reply—I had answers from Arsenal, Blackpool, Carlisle, Leicester, Luton, Milwall, Norwich, Notts Forest, Oxford and West Bromwich Albion. And out of these Carlisle had no apprentices or associate schoolboys on their books; Don Howe at WBA said bluntly 'I am not prepared to answer your questionnaire'; Leicester said they were 'getting so many requests of this nature that it was not possible to deal with them'; and Luton said that they had some bad experiences with people to whom they had given information in the past. The answers hardly give you confidence in football's careers advice service.

What the clubs said
(Figures given are averages of answers received.)

Number of associate schoolboys   **14**
How many likely to become apprentices?   **9**
Number of apprentices   **10**
What wages do they earn?   **Between £5 and £8 up to 17; between £5 and £10 up to 18.**
How many turn professional at 18?   **6**
Further education or vocational training for apprentices   **Optional 2 mornings at local college.**
Away from home where do apprentices live?   **In approved digs, or hostel, or with a family.**
What work do apprentices have to take on around the club?   **7 hours a week, cleaning the ground, tidying dressing rooms, etc.**
Why do so few apprentices make the grade?   **Failure to develop. Lack of skill. Homesickness. Lack of application.**

(university degrees) have carried on with their education to a later stage than most players, and have still broken in to top teams at a later age. This can mean a rather different attitude to offers of glory and fame from a club, as Steve Heighway remembers when told Bill Shankly was coming to see him:

'I was completely unimpressed. It was nothing to do with my life. Mr Shankly came and went on about all the money I'd get as a first-team player. I said, "Oh yes, but your reserve players, how much do they get?" He wouldn't talk about me being in the reserves.'

So the pattern of young players may change a little in the near future. But surely something more radical needs to be done to alter the basic structure which surrounds the young player during his early years in the game? How about a football school, along the lines of ballet and drama schools, where young players receive intensive coaching, training and match experience from an early age—say ten or eleven—while they continue to receive a normal education at the same time. Of course only a few would gain entry, but then fewer would be disappointed. There are obviously difficulties in putting such a proposal into practice—but are there any fundamental objections to it?

Changes of some kind are obviously urgently needed: but so is hard information on the pressures and strains, as well as the enjoyments, of a young footballer's life.

Graduate Steve Heighway shows his wife where he's learning another trade.

Scrap heap of broken dreams

LEN ASHURST, manager of Gillingham Football Club, is a hard man in a hard game.

I commend to all soccer-struck youngsters the essence of his attitude towards professional football as a career:

"Hundreds of young lads throughout the country are turned away disappointed and disillusioned.

"But if they have got guts in their bellies they will go elsewhere."

It is a blunt assessment of the youth schemes in which Football League clubs nourish the aspirations of promising lads in the hope of finding a rare talent.

It is a realistic attitude and a bitter one.

Take the case of Jimmy Cable, a 17-year-old goalkeeper who went for a trial with Gillingham in February.

The club were sufficiently impressed to invite him to join their youth squad and to train with them twice a week.

Seven months later Jimmy Cable has joined the ranks of the disappointed and disillusioned.

Why was Jimmy turned away?

"You had better talk to Bill Collins about that. He is the youth manager."

Mr. Collins remembered Jimmy Cable.

"He came to us," he said, "at the same time as two other goalkeepers and he looked the best of the three.

"So we asked him to train with us."

"It is difficult to assess a player in trials.

"You have to judge them against better opposition.

"But he seemed promising and it is true we signed him in August.

"Unfortunately, we had two other young goalkeepers coming through and I thought they looked better.

"So I advised Jimmy to go and play with his local club — and we would keep in touch.

"I try to avoid this kind of thing as much as possible, but we do not have talent scouts like the rich clubs so we have to rely on this kind of system.

Sorry son, no good

"Most of it is a waste of time, but I always tell the lads: 'Don't take our word for it. I'll cancel your forms and you can try your luck somewhere else. . . .'"

So that's it. You try your luck. That is the system.

All play and no work?

'To a certain extent, football is still like white slavery.' Billy Bremner, Leeds and Scotland

'How many transferred players cry all the way to church on Sunday with a thousand grand in their pockets?' Bob Lord, Chairman of Burnley

In July 1974 the Commission for Industrial Relations issued a report which made many criticisms of the way professional football is run. In particular it drew attention to the working conditions of the players of today, arguing that they compare unfavourably with those of workers in other kinds of employment. And it made it clear who its members thought were the villains of the piece:

'Our inquiries have shown that at all levels of the game relations between the players and their employers, and their respective representatives are unsatisfactory. Negotiating and consultative procedures function sporadically in England and Wales and are rudimentary in Scotland; at club level proper disciplinary and grievance procedures are often lacking, and their absence, together with inadequate collective discussion between players and managements about common terms and conditions of employment, sometimes leads to the destruction of mutual respect between players and managements....

The autocratic approach of some club representatives is ill advised. We say this directly because we believe that if the attitudes of some clubs do not change and if reforms in relation to the matters with which this report deals are not carried through, there is a danger that the professional game could be seriously dislocated and its future threatened.'

But is football really an occupation where we can talk about industrial relations? Does it make sense to think of Dave Thomas or Trevor Francis as a 'worker'? Isn't football essentially about excitement, risk, conflict, where players are required to adapt and respond to uncertainty? Maybe it's possible to get some kind of answer to these questions if we look at why players are drawn into the professional game, and what kind of pressures and rewards they meet once they make it into a League team.

'I didn't pay out £150 000 to let him sit on the touchline with a torn ligament.'

DUNCAN ON THE DOLE

£200-a-week star quits

By DAVE HORRIDGE

DUNCAN McKENZIE, Nottingham Forest's £250,000-rated striker, yesterday walked out on the club—and now faces life on the dole.

The latest twist in McKenzie's dispute over a reported £200-a-week contract ended with him asking for—and being given—his cards.

Corrigan says—'I must go'

JOE CORRIGAN (left) is determined to quit Manchester City. The 26-year-old goalkeeper will ask manager Tony Book for a transfer and if he doesn't get one he will pack up football altogether.

That's the result of the Maine Road crowd's attitude to Corrigan which he claimed last night " has brought me near to a mental breakdown."

" But now I've been driven out by a hostile crowd

'If they won't fight, they won't play..' —Spurs boss

TERRY NEILL, manager of Tottenham, takes his relegation-threatened team to Yugoslavia tomorrow for a friendly with Red Star in Belgrade.

They fly out knowing that Neill is ready to axe any player not prepared to fight for survival.

" Those who can't stand the heat—and there are one or two—will end up in the reserves." Neill warned.

" Most of my men are not used to being in this situation. Some of them are not used to working for a living. They will have to learn damn quickly or they will not play for me."

WHAT THEY EARN

DIVISION	I	II	III	IV
Less than £25 a week	9.7%	12.5%	11.0%	11.6%
£25 to £34 a week	23.8%	17.5%	18.0%	33.4%
£35 to £44 a week	10.7%	15.8%	43.6%	45.5%
£45 to £54 a week	9.7%	24.8%	17.2%	7.8%
£55 to £74 a week	16.5%	21.5%	8.1%	1.3%
£75 to £99 a week	17.2%	5.9%	1.7%	0.0%
£100 and upwards a week	12.4%	2.0%	0.4%	0.4%

Why they do it

Financial gain is not such a good argument as it may seem. Very few players ever go home with 'a thousand grand in their pockets'. Only the very successful players, who belong to the richest clubs and can expect regular bonuses and other incentives, could reasonably be described as highly paid. At the end of 1973 the average *basic* wage for the two thousand or so players in the Football League was just under £50 a week: this compares with the average national wage of £41 for manual workers at that time.

The chart based on the CIR's findings destroys a lot of the myths about footballers as rich men with money to throw around. You can choose your own statistics from this set of figures, but it's interesting to see, for example, that:
—90% of fourth division players earned less than £45 a week
—1 out of every 3 first division players received under £35 a week
—Only 12% of first division players brought in over £100 a week

Of course some players earn more money outside the game than in, by putting their names to products, running their own shops or businesses, getting paid for columns written for them in newspapers or magazines. But here again the CIR figures are surprising; it seems that no less than 85% of League players have no source of income outside the game. So it's not the money that attracts.

Many are drawn by the fame that goes with being an object of national or even only local attention; others undoubtedly see soccer as a job which offers an escape —from office, pit or factory. There may even be one or two players who go into the game principally to be able to test out their skills against the best in the land.

Probably a mixture of all these reasons lies behind the entry of most League players to the game, if we assume that

Ecstasy for Liverpool's Steve Heighway as he scores the winner against Luton . . . agony for Newcastle's Irving Nattrass after being injured in the first minute against Birmingham.

great thought and care goes into their choice of occupation. But football is a game that breeds fanaticism, and many players decide to try to get into the game while they are still comparatively young. In some cases, if we are to believe players' life stories, an obsession with the game and a desire to perfect certain skills appears at a very early age. Derek Dougan's case is typical of many.

'At the bottom of Avon Street was a patch of waste ground which we called 'the Meadow', and on Sundays we would be out there as early as nine o'clock in the morning. We would start with two or three on each side, and by lunchtime we probably had as many as twelve or thirteen a side. Then for the next two hours it fluctuated, with people (boys and even grown men) going for their dinner. This went on until dusk, and even beyond, so that sometimes the game lasted up to twelve hours. I would have to go to Sunday School for about a couple of hours. I would go home and change into my best clothes and then change back after Sunday School. Then I would dash back to the Meadow, where I would find the score something like 42 to 37. Such was my Sunday.' Derek Dougan, *The Sash My Father Wore*

An obsession can also be fixed on the local team. With the great Tommy Lawton it was a question of seeing the last ten minutes of Bolton's League match after himself having played in *two* Saturday matches. Emlyn Hughes provides a good modern example of this early dedication to what goes on at the local club.

'Dad always used to take us to watch Barrow, rugby and soccer, cricket matches, anything at all that was going on in the town, and we'd get totally involved in Barrow winning, no matter who they were playing. We were there solely for Barrow to win. I idolized Barrow. I used to travel all over. I did a round trip one day to Plymouth. We travelled down by train, me and my mate Derrick Davies, and it must have took us about nine hours getting there. We set off at about four in the morning, saw them get beat 4–1, and travelled back. For anyone to do that to watch Barrow, you've got to be totally committed.'

If a player is fortunate enough to make the grade, is his life in fact as thrilling and adventurous as some sports writers and most football magazines make out? Or is he in much the same kind of situation as other employees, except that once or twice a week he jumps into a pair of shorts and kicks a spherical object round a field with 21 other men?

... a public cuddle for scorer Jairzinho from Brazilian teammate Paulo Cesar ... despair from Liverpool's Kevin Keegan after missing a goal in the European Cup Winner's Cup first round.

Carlisle's Bobby Parker makes a lunging tackle to try to stop Chelsea's Chris Garland.

All work and no play?

'I talk about "going to work" and people laugh. They think you just kick a ball about on a Saturday afternoon, and that's your lot. It's special because you get attention from the public for doing it.' Steve Perryman, and other Spurs players questioned by Hunter Davies in *The Glory Game*, saw football in this way, as a rather special kind of job—but nevertheless a job. Certainly a professional today does more than just 'kick a ball about'. During a typical week of the season he will have to undergo four or five mornings' intensive training, either at the ground or at the club's training centre. He is expected to be punctual, and is likely to be fined unless he has a really convincing excuse. If he misses training he will probably face a suspension.

Not so long ago even some of the top clubs took a fairly casual attitude to training; when Derek Dougan joined Blackburn in 1960, a couple of laps of the ground was apparently a good morning's work. Nowadays there is plenty of practice and development of ball skills, but also a great emphasis on stamina and endurance. Many League players will recognize this fictional description by Terry Venables and Gordon Williams of the effects of sprint training (known as 'doggies') on a man who is less than match fit.

'... only forty yards to go, don't let it beat you, man—my arms are screaming with pain—keep going man, show them you can still do it—the post is running away from me, I can't breathe, the air's so cold it's burning my throat—my thighs are giving up, not another yard—

He ran past the post. His head was thumping and his eyes were hazy. He seemed to be moving in slow motion. Voices and faces came to him but he went on walking, as if to stop would mean to fall down, and he found himself behind the little wooden pavilion. He sank slowly to the ground, as if in a dream. Waves of blood pumped through his eyes. He crouched like an animal, on hands and knees, unable to move, body so pulverized he could not tell if he was going to be sick. Like a panting dog, he thought. For fifty quid a week.'

Taking the strain

'The list of pressures on professional footballers is endless. They exert pressures on themselves because of their own ambitions. Money, the bonuses they play for that can make all the difference to their standard of living, add to that weight. Their team mates put pressures on them, for football is a team game, and one man's failure may be a team's disaster. The coaches and managers put pressures on them because their success is tied to the player's performance. The club's directors, the crowds, even their own families exert pressures for their own reasons on the player. Everyone wants success for his or her team, but the buck stops with the player.' Neil Philips, medical officer of the FA

A German physiotherapist believes in the advantages of hanging injured players upside down!

Legs 'Got to bounce them a bit early on. Makes your job easier if they pack it in. That's half the threat gone, isn't it? I like them to have the ball early on and run across me. Then I can get in, take the ball and take them and all. Not a foul, just a whacking.' Norman Hunter, Leeds and England

Bum After Terry Mancini had bared his bum to the crowd during Queen's Park Rangers' match with Ipswich, the FA disciplinary committee thought the fine should depend on how far the player had lowered his shorts.

Head 'Constant heading may have its repercussions not in classic punch-drunk symptoms, but in degeneration of the nerve cells at the spinal column, a tendency to irritability, loss of memory and premature senility.' Nicholas Corsellis, neuropathologist

Pelvis 'The diagnosis was strained pelvic muscles. These muscles control so much —your running, your passing, your body movements, stopping, starting, everything.' Alan Mullery, Fulham and England

Brain 'Psychological techniques have been used to perfect skills, to ensure that moves come to mind spontaneously, to reduce emotional stress, and to avoid panic.' Maurice Yaffé, resident psychologist, Crystal Palace

Nose 'I was hit on the nose and it bled. I was taken to a room where I was made to kneel in a corner. I was punched eight or nine times and kicked twice. They didn't realize I was a footballer.' Kevin Keegan at Belgrade Airport's police room

'I'm like the rest of them now. I can't relax. It *must* be wrong. I've seen my doctor and he's suggested tranquilizers. I've refused them. I feel that would really be the end. But I need something.' Steve Heighway, Liverpool and Republic of Ireland

The working week of a player may be short compared with that of a factory worker or a wages clerk, but it is undoubtedly intense. Whether a team's performance would automatically fall apart if players were given a chance to plan their individual training schedules is a matter which has rarely been raised. Clearly a certain amount of group work is needed every week. However Jimmy Hill, with experience as both player and manager, said recently that he thought the majority of English players would be better if left to train alone. Nobody has really tested this theory yet; though during his fortnight's suspension in December 1974 Keith Weller kept fit by jogging around country lanes and doing his own fitness exercises, with no apparent loss of stamina or skill.

The overorganization and stressful conditions which professional players experience in up to 60 games a season, has opened up the Cup competitions to some surprising results. In 1975 Wimbledon beat Burnley and forced Leeds to a replay; Chester made it to the semi-final of the League Cup; Wycombe Wanderers held the then League leaders to a draw; and Leatherhead beat Brighton before losing by the odd goal after a great fight against Leicester. Brighton's manager, Peter Taylor, suggested that all was not well with the way League players were being handled.

'Leatherhead are a credit to the game. They won honestly, and when you consider most of their players go to work each day from around eight in the morning to five at night, it makes you wonder whether it would do some of our professional players good to do a day's work. Not just our lads, but all professionals.'

Off the ball

Clubs inevitably have their own ideas about how players should go about enjoying themselves. Chris Balderstone, who has played first-class county cricket as well as first-division League football, has had experience of the opposing attitudes to be found within the two sports:

'For cricket I am able to make my own preparations. I came to the club this morning and had ten minutes in the nets playing properly. Tomorrow if we're in the field I shall loosen up in the nets as I want. In football you've got to do what you're told. . . . You're under restriction in football, but not here. I'm not told to go to bed at a certain time and I'm not told to do five laps before I go out to bat. I know what suits me best and I do it.'

And then there's drink, gambling and sex. Or rather then there *isn't* drink, gambling and sex.

DRINK

Most clubs try to insist that players confine their drinking to Saturday nights, though a number of players reported to be living it up during the week seem to keep their place in the first team on Saturdays. Each manager has his own way of approaching this sensitive issue. At Stoke one player remarked that 'no one would know what the rules are if you asked him'; while Don Revie, when he was manager at Leeds, used to take his players every Friday to a country house for a bingo session, just to keep a 'fatherly' eye on them.
Look what happened in September 1975 when Billy Bremner and four other Scots Internationals had a few drinks in Copenhagen after a European Championship game. Though the police took no action, the Scottish FA immediately took the extreme step of banning the players for life from the International team, without attempting to hear the players' side of the story.

Are team managers justified, or even sensible, to try to keep a tight rein on the social activities of adults?

GAMBLING

Gambling is less of a headache, unless you have someone like Stan Bowles on your staff. In January 1974 he admitted: 'I don't seem to be able to beat the gambling bug. I've lost about £10 000 to the bookies over the years.' At Queens Park Rangers Bowles was becoming such a compulsive gambler that the club took over all his financial affairs and left him with £20 a week pocket money. The rest went direct to his wife, who looked after items such as mortgage repayments on their house.

But is a club acting fairly in interfering so drastically in a player's private life? Ernie Tagg, who once managed Bowles when he was with Crewe, remarked: 'If Stan Bowles could pass a betting shop like he can pass a ball he'd have no worries at all.' But if Stan Bowles has to sit quietly in his 'semi' every evening, will he retain that ability to be extravagantly daring and dramatic on the field, qualities which spectators have been so starved of these last few years?

SATURDAY MEN love their Sundays

Sunday's a day of rest for Gerry Francis—until the *Sunday Mirror* invades his sauna for a photo session.

SEX

As for sex, it has long been the custom for players to be instructed to 'Take it easy' the night before a match; meaning, cut it out. Some managers go further than this. In Italy the players are kept isolated on match night as well; while in England Don Revie recently declared that at Leeds he was 'a great talker on sex and getting the right sleep in, two nights before a match'. And yet no evidence has been produced to link one night's performance in bed with the next day's on the field. Perhaps the last word should be left with the doctor attached to the Dutch World Cup team, Fritz Kessel. On two occasions during the Munich finals the Dutch sent a plane to bring in wives and girl-friends ('But please not both' requested the manager'), who were allowed to spend the night with the players. Kessel commented: 'These are men, not monks—enforced celibacy can destroy a player's concentration.' Holland showed superb skills and energy during the competition, and were generally considered to have played the finest football.

'It's a club rule. We've got to wear pads.'

CLOUGH A FOOL—REVIE

No holds barred as former Leeds managers clash on TV

BRIAN CLOUGH could now apply for the job as manager to England's Youth team.

He admitted at the end of a stormy face-to-face meeting with his Leeds predecessor Don Revie on Yorkshire television early today that it was the one job which really appealed to him.

Socialist Clough also said that he was aiming for a soccer Utopia.

"Maybe I am a little bit stupid, a bit of an idealist. I do believe in fairies."

England boss Revie slammed Clough in no uncertain style.

Criticisms

REVIE opened up by saying "I feel truthfully Brian is a fool to himself.

"He has criticised Sir Matt Busby, me personally, Norman Hunter, Peter Lorimer, Billy Bremner, Peter Storey... criticised so many people in the game whose records stand to be seen.

"I think it is totally wrong in the game of professional football.

"He talks about honesty. If honesty is going to destroy the game you are doing the game a great disservice."

Asked why he had come to Leeds in the first place after criticising so many of the players, Clough answered: "It was the best job in the country. I was taking over the champions."

WHY I'VE QUIT

Cash meant more than my opinion with this board

I RESIGNED from Preston simply because I didn't want to stay where my opinion as manager didn't carry weight when the club were about to take what I considered to be a backward step.

Newcastle made an offer of either Micky Burns or Alex Bruce, plus some money, for our captain John Bird. I rate Bird as one of the best centre halves in the country and I wasn't keen on either of the players Newcastle offered.

BOBBY CHARLTON
who resigned yesterday as manager of Preston
talking to
ALEC JOHNSON

Who's in charge...the manager?

Managers need to be eternal optimists, says Joe Mercer. As an ex-England manager, he should know. It's a cliché to say that the manager has the most insecure job in football; he also has the most complicated one. In many clubs he is supposed to be a source of motivation for the players, a shrewd businessman, a talent scout, a master tactician, a father figure, a press officer, an accomplished administrator and a psychiatrist all rolled into one.

Even the best of modern managers haven't managed this combination. Ron Greenwood is a great tactician and a marvellous spotter of skill and creativity in a player—he signed Alan Taylor from Rochdale after scarcely having seen him touch the ball during 90 minutes—but he never quite fired his players with the highest ambitions. When John Lyall moved in under Greenwood, West Ham immediately captured the Cup, playing in the 1974/75 season with a purpose and fire previously missing. A new manager can often transform the fortunes of a club, perhaps even more than a new player. But even if he has the tactical know-how of Dave Sexton, the dynamism of Brian Clough, the aggressive bravado of Tommy Docherty or the coaching ability of Bobby Robson, in the end a manager's reputation depends on the performance of the players.

There's still a long way to go before managers strike the right personal balance in their working relationship with their team. Many still adopt paternalistic, over-protective or distant attitudes to the players. As a playe in the 1930s, Ted Drake could tell whether h would be staying on at his club only by the manager's positive or negative reaction to his end-of-season request for a new pair of boots In the 1970s Alfie Conn, having talked to bo the manager and chairman of Spurs, was still confused about whether they wanted him to carry on at White Hart Lane. Maybe he should have tried the boot test?

.... and who's in charge at the top?

Old guard who run the game

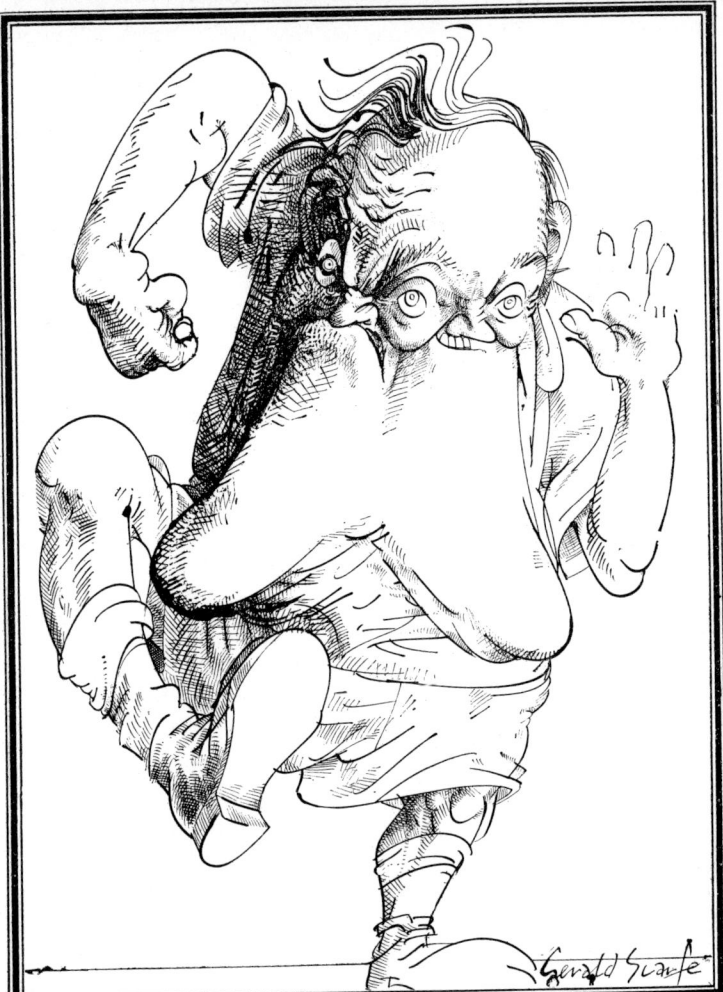

Two faces of Don Revie, the England manager.

'I told them to play it tight for a while. George just went out and destroyed them. I couldn't believe it. Out comes this kid as if he's never heard of tradition and starts running at them, turning them inside out. I ought to have shouted at him for not following instructions. But what can you say?' Matt Busby on George Best's performance in Manchester United's 5–1 defeat of Benfica.

THE nine men who run the Football League have an average age of sixty-four—and that figure would be much higher but for the presence of Charlton's Michael Gliksten, who is thirty-six.

The all-powerful Management Committee is made up of business men who built fortunes outside the game, then took their money with them on to football club boards.

The only exception is Sir Matt Busby, who followed his career as a Scotland international player with great success as manager of Manchester United.

An outspoken opponent of the committee is Derrick Robins, chairman of Coventry City. He said: "The people who run football have butchers shops and transport businesses and in their spare time like to look after football.

"They don't seem to take their business brains to Lytham St. Anne's. What football needs is a good managing director."

Who's in charge of the match...the referee?

Billy Bremner of Leeds disciplined by the referee.

'A referee is a man with his coat-collar up to hide his face, exposed in the spotlight at Checkpoint Charlie. He is a man with little social life, no friends in football, the man whose side of the story is never listened to, even at disciplinary commissions.' Alan Stewart, *Foul*

'The referee is controlling workers in an industry which works in a highly charged, emotional atmosphere, seeing that they do not kick lumps out of each other.' Norman Burtenshaw, League referee who retired in 1974

'There have always been players capable of losing their tempers, and there always will be. What worries me most is dissent. We are not going to clean up the game unless everyone wants to do it. And that means the clubs along with the rest of us. I have tried to adjust my game to the new instructions, but I have not discarded my principles. To me refereeing still means man management, unobtrusiveness and mutual respect.' Jack Taylor, World Cup Final referee, 1974

'They're still outside waiting for the ref, Sarge!'

PLAY GIRLS..

THE SEX EQUALITY Bill before Parliament is giving headaches to the men at Denis Howell's Ministry of Sport.

It could mean, for instance, that women would be entitled to referee men's Soccer matches.

Howell was himself a Football League referee for fourteen years.

A spokesman at his Ministry admitted yesterday: "This is a real hornets' nest.

"Lots of international federations stipulate that only men can take part in events."

The idea of women referees does not appeal to Soccer's Establishment.

"Our rules say no females can be in charge of men's games," roundly declares Reg Paine, 52, referees' secretary of the Football Association.

This doesn't cut much ice with Pat Gregory, secretary of the Women's Football Association.

"There is no reason why we should not referee men's games,' she says.

With the logic of the emotions which characterise women she adds: "Having women in charge would probably do men good. We don't cheat like they do."

Bingo between goalposts?

'I never used to think about the game. I just used to go out there and play; but the more I get to know about football, the more complications I get. Now I have too many instructions to cope with. I get frightened to go deep for the ball. I think, "No, I had better stay here, but in my mind I want to play everywhere . . . and be free." '

Peter Osgood is not the only one who thinks that football is losing one of its greatest assets: surprise. The game seems to have been taken over by the organization men, or by those who think merely in terms of results, and care nothing for the kind of play that achieves the results. Managers, and to a lesser extent directors, are in a game where most of them each year will not win anything. It's easier to play safe if you want to remain in the job. Yet do a club's supporters really prefer their team to lose brilliantly 4–3 every week, or to scrape a dreary 1–0 victory? All these pressures ultimately focus on the individual player. To the board of directors he is a hunk of capital; to the physiotherapist a mass of flesh and bones; to the manager, increasingly, a slave to team tactics and club requirements.

You would think that the kind of changes in method which took place in the early 1960s would have led to greater scope for the individual player. You were no longer a well-defined left half or inside-right, but more vaguely 'at the back', in midfield or 'up front'. In practice,

All change

Everybody has their own idea of what is wrong with football just now. On the face of it there wouldn't seem to be much difficulty in getting certain laws altered. But every proposal for change will have its opponent, whether it be player, manager, director, referee, administrator, supporter. What would you think of the suggestions below as answers to some of our current football problems? Would you oppose them, and if you didn't who do you think might?

Problem Defensive football, particularly playing for an away draw, is ruining the excitement in football. **Solution** Alter the points system so that there is a greater reward for winning, and for scoring more goals. Why not points as follows: none for a defeat, 1 for a goalless draw, 2 for a score draw, 5 for a win, and a further point for each goal scored in a victory?

Problem Players deliberately waste time when their team is ahead, to the frustration of the crowd. This is done when the ball is out of play as much as when it is in. The ball is actually only in play for about 60 of the 90 minute period. **Solution** Allow for one hour's playing time, and stop the clock whenever the ball is out of play.

Problem Far too often a player will bring down an opponent when he is the last line of defence before the goal. Some brilliant solo efforts have been stopped by this method. **Solution** If the foul is outside the penalty area, award a penalty anyway and book the player. If it's inside the area, award the penalty but send the player off too.

Problem It is almost impossible for a new team to get into the League, since the four teams seeking re-election each year invariably get the vote of the other league clubs at the annual meeting. **Solution** Make relegation automatic, and elect to the League the champions from the four strongest competitions outside the League. Relegated teams would have the chance to return, but on merit.

Problem The number of fouls remains high. It is still rare for a player to be sent off, referees being reluctant to use the ultimate weapon too often. **Solution** If a player commits more than one foul, he should sit on the trainer's bench for five minutes. If he offends again on his return, the suspension time is doubled; the same applies for each additional offence.

Problem There are too many fixtures: players with successful clubs can play up to sixty matches a year. **Solution** Increase the number of divisions, with fewer clubs, say sixteen, in each. Make the two lower divisions on a regional basis, to save travelling expenses and time for the remote clubs at either end of the country.

every player was expected to be enough of an all-rounder to operate in a variety of positions during the course of a single game. No more wingers running up and down the touchline, or centre forwards waiting in the centre circle for the inside forwards to bring them the ball. Though the player was still called a player, and not a worker, he seemed to have become a victim to the idea of 'work-rate', subject to 'formation square-bashing' known as 4—2—4 or 4—4—2. Or as Geoffrey Green has nicely put it: 'The game's not much fun any more. It's all Penguin football, bingo between goalposts.'

However, if the situation seemed restrictive in England, Denis Law found things much worse in Italy during his few months there:

'Honestly, you would be bored to tears by the dreary, slogging, slow-motion stuff dished up most weeks in Italy under the guise of football. From the forwards' point of view, a game consists of one long battle of wits with the defence, trying to lure just one defender out of position to create an opening. And at the first sign of danger the whole of the opposing team will funnel back in defence and bolt the door.'

Today there has perhaps been some

Coach talk is rubbish —Mackay

DAVE MACKAY marked his arrival at the pinnacle of English football with an outspoken attack on the system he has defied to win the League Championship for Derby.

In a bold statement of his philosophy Mackay yesterday called for the game to be taken away from the stereotype influence of coaches and given back to a public waiting to be entertained.

Mackay broke off from celebrations which had seen the morning-after merge with the night-before to say 'Coaches are making a simple game difficult, trying to turn players into robots.

'To hear some of them talk you would think you need ten 'A' levels before you can play or understand how to play.

'They use mystical phrases and involved theories and formations—and most of it is absolute rubbish.

'We are beginning to hear players say the manager will give them a rocket because they scored a goal when they shouldn't have been in that position. What a joke.

'What worries me more is that the negative influence is spreading. I recently saw an England under-15 team playing with a sweeper.

It almost made me cry because, although they won 5-0, they would have got ten without the sweeper.

movement away from the rigidity of many of these tactics, though it's a little premature, to say the least, to talk of 'Total Football', as if, overnight, every player on the field will be searching for a goal before all else. However, the 1974 World Cup did show that when a talented team decides to play attacking football it can generate highly imaginative and exciting movements. David Lacey in the *Guardian* looked at Holland's performance in the final stages, two days before they were due to meet West Germany in the Final:

'Underlying all the Dutch successes has been the theme of flexibility. The words "forward" and "defender" have little meaning in their system. Immediately a player gains possession he is in an attacking situation, even if he is near one of his own corner flags. The men at the back have the skill of creative players, the pace and accuracy of strikers, those up front can cover and double cover in an emergency. The capacity for work is remarkable.'

On whose terms?

If you've been employed in the holidays, or you're already in a permanent job, you'll have noticed the difference between how it seems before you start, and how it is a little while later. Contracts or a letter of employment, if you get one, usually hide more than they tell. Have you ever tried writing an *honest* account of your job in the form of a letter of contract? Here are a few clauses that *might* appear in a professional footballer's contract. Allowing for the difference in style, how many do you think appear in an *actual* contract?

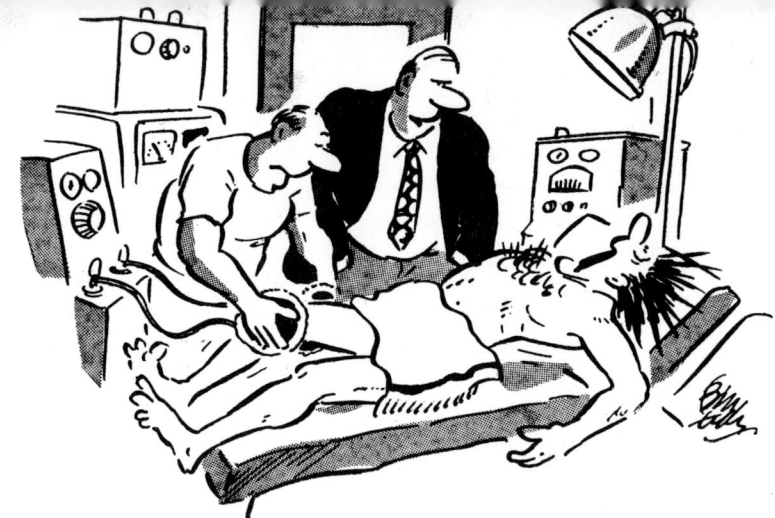

'Look Jock, withdraw your transfer request and we'll all be friends again.'

1. **The Player hereby agrees** to play efficiently according to the instructions of his manager and coach, and not to question the wisdom or knowledge of said officials of the club.

2. **The Player hereby agrees** that after a year if the club wishes to renew the contract for a further period they may do so; but that if the Player wants to stay for that period and the club doesn't want him, he be shown the door.

3. **The Player hereby agrees** not to live anywhere which the club feels might offer him too much temptation or harm the image of the club.

4. **The Player hereby agrees** to go to bed early, avoid night clubs, spend most of the year in coaches, trains, airport or hotels, and be satisfied with cards, bingo and television as leisure activities.

5. **The Player hereby agrees** to stand by the directors' judgement when and if they appoint a new manager, and not to expect to be asked if he approves of the man with whom he will have to work closely for 46 weeks of the year.

6. **The Player hereby agrees** that he will not talk to, or take up the pen as, a newspaper writer without asking the club if he may do so, and if it agrees to the latter then every word must be approved by the club.

7. **The Player hereby agrees** to put up with being called 'boy', 'lad' or 'servant of the club', and to always call the manager 'the Boss', and accept his proper place in the club cheerfully.

8. **The Player hereby agrees** that if the club wishes to transfer him they will consult almost everyone else before letting him in on the secret.

9. **The Player hereby agrees** that the club has no responsibility to do anything for him once his playing days are over, since there is only room for 1 in 10 to get a job within the game.

The player and his union

1898 Led by players from Manchester United, the Union of Professional Footballers is founded. It later changes its name to the Professional Footballers Association.

1909 League refuse to allow Union to be recognized by Federation of Trade Unions. Players eventually threaten strike action, and clubs sign sufficient amateur players to get them through their first fixtures. Two days before season begins Union granted recognition.

1952 Negotiations on pay and conditions between League and Union reach deadlock. Ministry of Labour investigating committee recommend higher maximum wage, match bonuses, and legal representation for players in disciplinary matters. But efforts to obtain freedom for player to move at his own request, and for abolition of maximum wage, both fail.

1961 After threat of strike action and intervention by the Ministry of Labour, League give way three days before strike due to begin, and allow abolition of maximum wage.

1963 George Eastham takes his club Newcastle to the High Court, claiming that their refusal to grant his wish for a transfer was 'an unreasonable restraint of his trade'. Eastham's defence counsel refers to the system as being like the bartering of cattle, and a relic from the Middle Ages. Backed by the PFA as a test case, Eastham wins.

197? Players secure freedom of contract. Foreign players are allowed to register for British clubs.

The call for strike action in the 1960/61 season: Jimmy Hill chairs a PFA meeting.

Servants of the club

The players' union, the Professional Footballers' Association, has had a hard struggle to get to its present position. But it has gradually—despite apathy amongst a majority of players—improved the working conditions of its members. It has secured the freedom for players to move at their own request, and the abolition of the maximum wage, at a time when players could be paid no more than £20 a week. The PFA's next battle, which looks as if it could well be won at any moment now, is over the issue of freedom of contract, a situation that already exists in several European countries. At present a club holds a one-year option on a player's services after the contract has expired, which means that he can be prevented from playing for another club during that period. If the PFA have their way a player will be able to change clubs as soon as their agreement runs out. It's not a straightforward issue, but such a change would probably make a player's life a little easier, though it wouldn't necessarily reduce transfer fees at a stroke.

Meanwhile, a few players have acted in defiance of their masters, and placed their own feelings above loyalty to club or country. In 1974–75, when Stan Bowles and Kevin Keegan truanted from the England squad and Kevin Beattie went home to mum rather than join the Under 23 team in Scotland, Keith Weller's action was perhaps the most significant in relation to a player's freedom of action. After being jeered by the crowd during the first half of Leicester's home match with Ipswich in December 1974 Weller refused to come out of the dressing room for the second

Truants in boots: Stan Bowles and Kevin Beattie (left) and Kevin Keegan

half. A week before the club had refused his transfer request: after the incident they fined him £300 and—put him on the transfer list. That's one way of getting what you want, though many people may not consider it a reasonable one.

The press were heavily critical of Weller's action, as they usually are when a player steps out of line. But their reaction was mild compared to that of John Bond, the Norwich manager, who suggested that Weller should be blacklisted by other clubs for what he had done. His comment is worth looking at in detail:

'There should be no way that any manager can buy Weller after what he has done. He has completely undermined the authority of the Leicester manager. We were talking at a recent managers' meeting about solidarity. Well, here's a chance for all the managers to unite and show they will not be a party to anything like this . . . .

We must establish just who is running the football clubs. There can only be one answer: the managers must be in charge. If Weller is allowed to get away with this there is nothing to stop any other player who fancies a move doing exactly the same thing if he knows that other clubs will be straight in for him. Footballers are the worst people in the world for feeling sorry for themselves and if we don't stamp hard on this sort of action there is no knowing where it will all end. In my letter to the managers I will be asking them not to buy Weller at any price, to show that we are not prepared to let footballers call the tune, however talented they may be.'

Weller eventually came off the transfer list and helped Leicester avoid relegation that season, so he never became a test case.

The clear message of Bond's remarks is that, whatever new contractual freedoms the players win, they will still be subjected to treatment and comment which makes them, quite literally, 'servants of the club'. Considering how important a player's frame of mind is if he is to perform successfully, it is astonishing what sort of relationship exists between players and officials, particularly managers.

Duncan McKenzie's experience at Notts Forest sums up the kind of communication and consideration that exists. After McKenzie had turned up for an interview with Alan Brown to discuss a dispute over a pay rise, he found that the manager had gone off on a holiday. On telephoning his manager, McKenzie was told by Brown that he wanted to watch the Open golf tournament and wouldn't be back for a week! McKenzie had guts enough to take his cards, and was then signed up by Brian Clough during his lightning visit to the Leeds manager's office. If this is how a star player is looked after by his employers, how are the players of less value to a club being treated?

'Poor devil. He's having to sell his England caps one by one . . . .'

Not quite the thing

'I'd love to referee a women's match, but they won't let me bath with them.'
Malcolm MacDonald, Newcastle and England

More often than not, any mention of women playing football provokes either disbelief or merriment—usually from males. And suggestions that girls and women might enjoy watching a game soon turn the discussion to the kind of language that can be tolerated on the terraces. How far are these attitudes justified?

The long haul

Women have in fact been playing football for almost as long as men, though no one has been able to establish exactly when the first all-female game took place. One of the earliest must have been that played at Midlothian in Scotland on Shrove Tuesday. Here the wives were matched against the unmarried. Without the classified Saturday night paper the result must remain uncertain, but the story goes that the married players nearly always put one over on the unwed.

It's quite probable that isolated matches were played between the twelfth and nineteenth centuries, though there is virtually no record of them. But once the men had started to regularize the rules of the game, form committees, and assume a measure of self-importance, they soon issued an official announcement about women's football. Just before the turn of this century, the still young Football Association sent a stern note to clubs:

'Complaints have reached our ears that women are holding football matches. The FA is of the opinion that this game is totally unsuited to women and that they must not be encouraged.'

However, there was no law to prevent women from playing, and the FA were never really able to enforce their ruling, particularly where charitable causes were involved. During the First World War a ladies' club was formed to raise money for wounded servicemen in hospital. Their first match was played in 1917 on Preston's ground and attracted 10 000 spectators, a higher attendance figure than most third division clubs manage today.

Players of the Amazon Athletic Club in the nineteenth century, and of the England team in the twentieth.

The fight for the freedom of women to play football at club level was a long one: in 1946, for example, the FA was still urging its members 'to take steps to prevent clubs letting their grounds or otherwise creating opportunities for female players to participate in irregular football matches.' But now they have been able to form a Women's FA (complete with a male life president), they have a grant from the Sports Council and a sponsored Cup competition; and over 200 amateur regional teams throughout the country. As their secretary puts it: 'You men are just going to have to learn that you can't have everything.'

Perhaps the day of the female professional footballer is not all that far away. But how far will men and boys need to change their attitude to women playing the game? Consider the following:

1. In 1969 the acting organizing secretary of the Ladies Football Association was a man. He commented: 'It is a great joy to work and play with them—if you see what I mean.'

2. The present manager of the English women's team tells the women at training sessions to 'C'mon lads.'

3. England's lady right back Margaret Miks' boyfriend, a referee, 'takes her as seriously as she takes football'.

4. At a recent England v. France women's international a record of Maurice Chevalier singing 'Thank Heaven for Little Girls' was played over the loudspeaker.

Lost opportunities

Even if attitudes do change, schools will have to revise their ideas about hockey or netball being the only suitable game for girls. Many girls at primary school level might be interested in the game if they were offered access to both school teams and games periods. In the junior school where I taught the most skilful and intelligent player was a girl. She was tolerated as a curiosity, and valued because she was good at the game, but would she have been playing if her talents were only average; and what happens when she moves to secondary school?

Going back even further, perhaps we ought to look at the way pre-school boys and girls learn what to do with a football. Once they start to walk, *all* children seem to enjoy kicking a ball: yet by four or five you rarely see a girl or group of girls booting a ball around a park or open space. Are they following their 'natural' instincts, or the advice of mum or dad who reckon that football is 'not nice' for girls?

Language fit for ladies?

As for watching the game, despite all the agitation by the authorities about 'shielding the fairer sex from some of the words used on the terraces', women and girls still seem to turn up to my local First Division club in the same sort of numbers as they used to ten or fifteen years ago. Pictures of matches played at the Oval towards the end of the nineteenth century show more than a sprinkling of female spectators, despite the fact that even then the occasional naughty word could be heard coming out of the crowd. The loss of Queen's Park's unbeaten home record in 1876 appears to have loosened a few tongues:

'Yelling, hooting, and calling out the players by cognomens were nothing compared to the coarse and vulgar pleasantries indulged in. Happily no ladies were present in the vitiated atmosphere.'

Though the glasses suggest the women's game might be less rough than the men's, most of the 36 teams at this world tournament in Germany in 1973 had players injured.

But maybe women are not quite so upset by such matters as men seem to think they are? Perhaps they even enjoy hurling abuse at sporting events as much as the male sex? The writer George Orwell had something to say about this question as a result of his experience during the Second World War.

'A boxing audience is always disgusting, and the behaviour of the women in particular is such, that the army, I believe, does not allow them to attend its contests.... When Home Guards and regular troops were holding a boxing tournament, I was placed on guard at the door of the hall, with orders to keep the women out.'
George Orwell, 'The Sporting Spirit'

2-4-6-8! What do they communicate?

'It was when old ladies who had been coming in to my greengrocer's for years started talking about sweepers-up and creating space that I really understood the influence of television.' Jack Taylor, World Cup referee, 1974

Like it or not, most of us nowadays have come to rely pretty heavily on television, radio and the newspapers for the information we need to carry on our daily lives. This seems to apply to football as much as any other activity. Where would we be without the pre-match gossip passed on to us by football journalists; the edited highlights on our TV channels; the match reports in the press the next morning? Where? Well, we'd be back to a time when you knew what happened at a game because you went to it, or you depended on a friend to tell you about it after the event. Were they the good old days, or are millions of people now given a real chance to experience the excitement of football by means of someone else's pen, voice or camera?

Television

Television has brought football bang into the middle of the English home. Saturday night out has changed to Saturday night in, face to face with Match of the Day. Sunday dinners now reach their last course a little earlier than usual, to allow a finish in time for the Big Match programme. We can see if the top performers have washed their hair, we can follow their lips as they tell the referee what they think of his decisions. We are able to relive the 'highlights' of the game, fourteen times, in slow motion, from behind the goal, and perhaps before long, from inside the goalkeeper's shorts. And then we can be instructed about what *really* happened by listening to the words of wisdom of ageing players, or managers judged to have a good screen personality. But, in the end, do these programmes tell us how football really is, or do they simply turn it into yet another branch of light entertainment?

Brian Moore, who chairs The Big Match programme, is probably speaking for the policy of both channels when he says:

'Football on TV on a Sunday afternoon is an entertainment. I have a duty to my employers to present as entertaining a programme as possible—not just for committed football fans but for the guy in the street and for Mum.'

But is it only committed fans who worry about the way a match turns out on television? If we're only given half an hour or so from a ninety-minute match, can we really get to grips with the way in which it develops? We're obviously going to miss out on the 'lowlights' of the game, which is very often the time a team can take or lose control. And some players can be virtually edited out of the game, simply because their presence has been greatest during the part cut from the programme.

Furthermore, by concentrating so much on goalmouth incidents, and by running such competitions as 'Goal of the Month', television has tended to turn the game into a kind of ritualized target practice. And if nobody gets a bull's-eye, they can even change the programme. This happened in September 1973, after a scoreless draw between Leeds and Manchester United. London Weekend decided after the game to switch to another match, because the Elland Road game had not proved exciting enough. 'If United went there with a nine-man defence and got a point, then I think it's better not to show it,' said Brian Moore.

But do we have to accept *edited* games? It certainly seems crazy that some Scandinavian countries receive Match of the Day live on Saturday afternoon, while those living where the match is being played have to wait until the evening. Of

course clubs are justified in worrying about numbers at the turnstiles if a game is to be televised live. But they could do worse than look at Derek Dougan's idea of bringing one top match forward from Saturday to Thursday every week, and giving it live treatment. The clubs could be compensated if necessary, but weekend football would be unaffected—and untelevised.

Given all the vested interests involved, it's not very likely that the restrictions on televising anything other than the Cup Final and the Home Internationals live will be lifted. But maybe there are other ways in which the football programmes could be shaken up. For instance:

* Do we have to see the same presenters and experts every week?
* Wouldn't it be more satisfying to see one match only?
* What about after-match discussions between supporters, filmed on a train, in a pub, or just in the street after a game?
* How about some argument, between players, fans, directors, managers, coaches, about issues both on and off the field?
* What about mixing or even replacing the panel of experts with knowledgeable and involved supporters of the teams being televised?

There are more ways of putting together a TV football programme than the present tired formula suggests. Next time the BBC or ITV ask for your postcard naming the winner of Throw-In of the Month, try sending instead your own ideas on how their programmes should be organized.

Just look at who's been axed by ITV... ...and who is joining their Cup Final team

BRIAN CLOUGH

MALCOLM ALLISON

GARY GLITTER

BILL ODDIE

BRIAN CLOUGH, one of the most controversial voices on television has been axed by ITV as part of a big FA Cup Final shake-up, writes Michael Hart.

In fact, ITV have sacked their entire football panel, which over the last five years has also featured big names like Malcolm Allison, Derek Dougan, Jackie Charlton and Pat Crerand.

Clough, the Nottingham Forest manager formerly with Leeds, Brighton and Derby, became a national figure through the TV panel. He is now one of the most impersonated personalities on television.

Instead of the panel, ITV have three England players as guests for their Wembley coverage—Arsenal and England captain Alan Ball, Liverpool's Kevin Keegan, who scored twice in last year's Final, and Newcastle's Malcolm Macdonald, England's five-goal hero against Cyprus.

ITV's coverage on Saturday week starts at 11 a.m. and other big names joining commentator Brian Moore include comedian Freddie Starr, disc jockey Ed Stewart, pop singer Gary Glitter and "Goodie" Bill Oddie.

Who would you want to see on the panel? Given the style of presentation, would it really make much difference?

The Press

Apart from what *kind* of football, there's also the question of how *much* football. During the Munich Finals in 1974 the TV companies gave very extensive coverage over a three-week period. This, in a country whose team had been knocked out of the competition the previous winter—as the *Sun* made quite clear to its readers the morning after England's defeat by Poland.

What do the newspapers tell us about football? Most people would rate accurate match reports pretty high on the list of requirements. But take a look at your paper next Sunday, and ask yourself what you are really getting. Too often the report revolves round a sensational incident, such as a penalty or a sending-off, with the details of the rest of the game left to the last paragraph. Or sometimes the reporter will appear to be concentrating more on the brilliance of his own style than on any skills on show on the pitch. Arthur Hopcraft himself a football writer, has commented

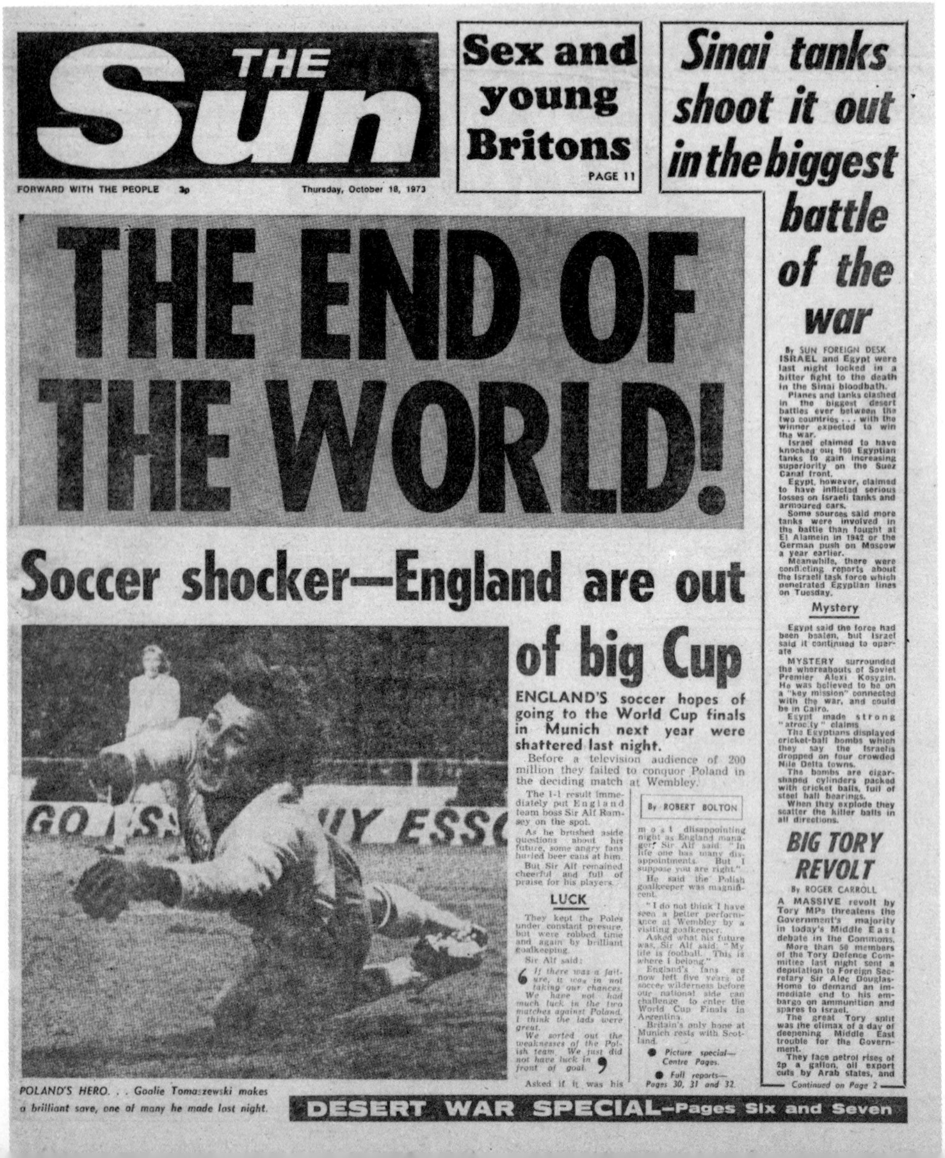

THE Sun

FORWARD WITH THE PEOPLE 3p Thursday, October 18, 1973

Sex and young Britons

PAGE 11

Sinai tanks shoot it out in the biggest battle of the war

By SUN FOREIGN DESK

ISRAEL and Egypt were last night locked in a bitter fight to the death in the Sinai bloodbath.

Planes and tanks clashed in the biggest desert battles ever between the two countries . . . with the winner expected to win the war.

Israel claimed to have knocked out 100 Egyptian tanks to gain increasing superiority on the Suez Canal front.

Egypt, however, claimed to have inflicted serious losses on Israeli tanks and armoured cars.

Some sources said more tanks were involved in the battle than fought at El Alamein in 1942 or the German push on Moscow a year earlier.

Meanwhile, there were conflicting reports about the Israeli task force which penetrated Egyptian lines on Tuesday.

Mystery

Egypt said the force had been beaten, but Israel said it continued to operate

MYSTERY surrounded the whereabouts of Soviet Premier Alexi Kosygin. He was believed to be on a "key mission" connected with the war, and could be in Cairo.

Egypt made strong "atrocity" claims

The Egyptians displayed cricket-ball bombs which they say the Israelis dropped on four crowded Nile Delta towns.

The bombs are cigar-shaped cylinders packed with cricket balls, full of steel ball bearings.

When they explode they scatter the killer balls in all directions.

BIG TORY REVOLT

By ROGER CARROLL

A MASSIVE revolt by Tory MPs threatens the Government's majority in today's Middle East debate in the Commons.

More than 50 members of the Tory Defence Committee last night sent a deputation to Foreign Secretary Sir Alec Douglas-Home to demand an immediate end to his embargo on ammunition and spares to Israel.

The great Tory split was the climax of a day of deepening Middle East trouble for the Government.

They face petrol rises of 2p a gallon, oil export cuts by Arab states, and

Continued on Page 2

THE END OF THE WORLD!

Soccer shocker—England are out of big Cup

GO ... ESSO

POLAND'S HERO . . . Goalie Tomaszewski makes a brilliant save, one of many he made last night.

ENGLAND'S soccer hopes of going to the World Cup finals in Munich next year were shattered last night.

Before a television audience of 200 million they failed to conquor Poland in the deciding match at Wembley.

By ROBERT BOLTON

The 1-1 result immediately put England team boss Sir Alf Ramsey on the spot.

As he brushed aside questions about his future, some angry fans hurled beer cans at him.

But Sir Alf remained cheerful and full of praise for his players.

LUCK

They kept the Poles under constant presure, but were robbed time and again by brilliant goalkeeping.

Sir Alf said:

'If there was a failure, it was in not taking our chances. We have not had much luck in the two matches against Poland. I think the lads were great.

We sorted out the weaknesses of the Polish team. We just did not have luck in front of goal.'

Asked if it was his most disappointing night as England manager, Sir Alf said: "In life one has many disappointments. But I suppose you are right."

He said the Polish goalkeeper was magnificent.

"I do not think I have seen a better performance at Wembley by a visiting goalkeeper."

Asked what his future was, Sir Alf said: "My life is football. This is where I belong."

England's fans are now left five years of soccer wilderness before our national side can challenge to enter the World Cup Finals in Argentina.

Britain's only hope at Munich rests with Scotland.

● Picture special—Centre Pages.

● Full reports—Pages 30, 31 and 32.

DESERT WAR SPECIAL—Pages Six and Seven

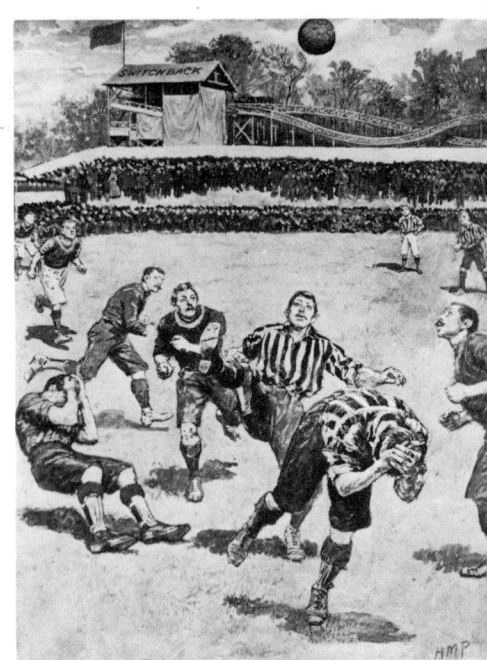

No action replay in pre-photographic times. This match in 1895 had an artist to reconstruct a highlight. The caption goes: 'Before half time, after a fierce bully for the ball, Devey, the centre-forward of the Villa and Higgins, the West Bromwich half-back, came violently into collision. Both of them reeled back with their hands to their heads and after swaying for a moment, Higgins suddenly sat down!'

Did the match of the day at Sinai get the right coverage?

on the 'foreign' language used by reporters.

'It is curious that football reporters very seldom use the same language in talking about the game that they employ when writing about it. No reporter has ever in his life stood with his back to the bar and a pint of bitter in his hand and said in all seriousness that a forward line moved as if Younger than Springtime, or that an inside-forward was a little general with dynamite in his boots.'

A notable example of this kind of writing was provided by Peter Batt in the *Sun*, reporting on West Germany's World Cup win in 1974. Under the near-hysterical headline 'The World Weeps for Holland: They Broke down the Barriers and Tore at my Heartstrings', he wrote paragraphs such as this:

'I can't speak for the rest of you, but it was the Dutch who found the lost chord in my heartstrings. Maybe it was just the natural pity one feels for losers anywhere, but a tiny country with a population of only 13 million was destined to have a tear or two of a start on most of the others anyway. The fact that they had painted rainbows on countless coloured television sets this past month did not do them any harm either. Inevitably then, when their bright orange shirts bent lower and lower like wilting sunflowers as the German victors did cartwheels all around them, some of us felt a surge of pity that was genuinely painful.'

Or this:

'During this unforgettable ninety minutes, when a man punched the air he was not putting up two fingers to his bank manager, he was reaching out to shake hands with his Maker, giving thanks for the flow of adrenalin that propelled him on to the greatest sporting stage on earth.'

Of course we prefer reporters to go beyond the level of 'United's second goal

---

David Lacey on Leeds United's release of their manager

Now Giles is set to succeed Clough

Brian Clough is no longer manager of Leeds United and the club are expected to appoint Johnny Giles as his successor today. Last night, 43 days after his arrival at Elland Road and 48 hours after a reported revolt in the dressing room, Clough agreed to part company with Leeds and will receive generous compensation.

Jago is obvious choice to take the England job

Gunners line up sale for Shilton

By BOB DRISCOLL

ARSENAL'S shock transfer - listing of Charlie George and Jeff Blockley could end their long wait for £350,000 England keeper Peter Shilton.

Jimmy Armfield succeeded Clough. Peter Shilton moved to Stoke. Don Revie was appointed England manager. Cruyff re-signed for Barcelona.

CRUYFF FOR ARSENAL!

That's Johan's target for next season

By LESLIE VERNON

JOHAN CRUYFF, the greatest footballer in the world, could be playing in the Football League next season—with Arsenal.

came from a free kick in the dying minutes of the game, when their burly centre forward (now striker) rose above the City defence to nod the ball home.' But there are writers who can combine imagination and style with an informative account of a match. Take Hugh McIlvanney's account of Scotland's game against Brazil a few days before that final:

'Hay was miserably adrift, like a man trying to pick up litter in a gale, during those first twenty minutes, in which the extraordinary failure to anticipate that Jairzinho would operate on the right wing plunged the Scots defence into calamitous disorder. Before the necessary adjustments had been made Scotland might have been three goals down and Hay might have been chronically sickened by his exhausting, unrewarded efforts to impose a steadying will on the confusion. Fortunately the excellent Harvey's goal stayed intact and Hay refused to be broken. He managed instead to drive his influence into the heart of the match, providing a rod of steel to conduct the creative electricity that had been flowing so brilliantly from Bremner almost from the start. Between them they lifted the team to a level of performance that fully deserved to claim victory in the second half.'

I happened to be standing behind David Harvey's goal during the first half of that Frankfurt game. Reading that account of the opening period of the game reminds me of the desperation of the Scots in those early minutes. It also makes clearer, by a clever spotlighting of the game through one player's performance, the part that a simple tactical switch played in the Brazilians' opening attacks. Football writing at its best, perhaps: vivid and helpful. Mind you, if you have to report matches twice a week throughout the season, it's quite a job to find an original angle. The football reporter's day has a predictability about it, like most people's routine. Frank Keating of the *Guardian* sees it this way:

'Winter reporting is a convivial British Rail brown-ale chat, all harmless 4–3–3, what-Bill-Nick-said-to-me transfer gossip, 300 deathless words on the whistle, accepting the consensus on who actually scored, time even for a finger of Scotch and a flaming-daylight-robbery-it-was-and-you-can-quote-me from the ashen-faced, tight-lipped supremo of the squad, and still ample time for the 5.40 buffet car to Euston, and back in your pit in time for Rugby Special, or at least the beginning of Cilla.'

Still, match reports only provide a part of the coverage that newspapers give to football. Many papers give over a large amount of space to rumours, gossip and speculation—possible transfers, shock team changes, dramatic injuries to key players, and so on. How many of these stories are invented merely to fill a space, or to do a public relations job for the coming week's fixtures?

Are there no other aspects of the game that the football writer can deal with? Or will his editor say that 'We're already printing the sort of things our readers want'? It's worth remembering that reporters, in the nature of their job, cannot afford to be on bad terms with the clubs whose games they will cover during a season, since they depend on them for such basic facilities as space, seating and shelter. At the same time, it pays managers and other club officials to spend a little time and effort on keeping reporters happy, since they act, deliberately or otherwise, as some of the best publicity agents the clubs will ever find.

England manager Don Revie quickly

Where your 50p gate money goes..

70%	10%	5%	4%	4%	4%	3%
Players' wages and requisites: 35p	Travel, hotel and match expenses: 5p	Ground expenses, police, referee, linesmen, medical expenses: 2½p	Rates and rent, lighting, heating, water and cleaning: 2p	Administration, postage, printing, telephones, staff wages billposting, : 2p	Interest and depreciation: 2p	Repairs and renewals: 1½p

A CUNNING GIRL'S GUIDE TO THE CUP FINAL

to know London .nis year. wearing k and white t, white k shorts with wn the side

ill run on in white shorts with sky blue and claret shirts. If you haven't got a colour TV set or a good memory, just remember Fulham are the black bottoms and West Ham are the pale tails.

Around 100,000 people will pack into Wembley stadium to watch the final. And 20 million more will see it on television.

To you it may be 90 minutes of utter boredom. But to your man it's a battle of the giants. And a clash between East and West.

That's because Fulham are the trendies from the posh Chelsea area of London, while West Ham is way over in London's East End. And to the toughest, smartest men goes the victory.

And even if you don't understand the action, the players will make great viewing. This year we will see the two handsomest teams who ever met for a Cup Final.

And Fulham probably have a slight edge over their rivals here. They've got gorgeous **Viv Busby.** He's 24, a sexy six footer with blue eyes and a dark

West Ham's goalie is 19 years old **Mervyn Day.** He looks slender, baby-faced and in need of a nice girl to cuddle him. But don't be fooled. You don't play in his position unless you're tough.

Different styles of reporting . . .

. . . footballer glamour in an office-girl magazine.

AIR-PLAY LEAGUE

EXPECTED, Liverpool and Chelsea hed their respective ends of the ent Fair-Play League. Chelsea ted home by nearly 100 points to them a marvellous double — releg- and the title of "dirtiest team rly) in the first division".

iverpool finished their season in , by conceding just 10 points at e to QPR. Before the game, they presented with the Fair-Play hy by League Secretary Alan aker. *Foul* readers may remember aker's ill-tempered letter in issue n which he revealed considerable ncern for what Trident were trying . He wrote:

. . I have to inform you that the nt Television Fair-Play League was uted without any prior consultat- ith the Football League, nor do I ony knowledge of the prizes great all which they are offering." e presumes that his presence at

		Played	Free-kicks (1pt)	Penalties (5pts)	Bookings (10pts)	Sendings Off (25pts)	Total points
1.	Liverpool	42	430	6	9	0	550
2.	Carlisle United	42	496	1	9	0	591
3.	Newcastle United	42	545	4	18	0	745
4.	Coventry City	42	561	4	19	1	796
5.	Leicester City	42	633	5	14	0	798
6.	Sheffield United	42	502	5	25	1	802
7.	Tottenham Hotspur	42	543	5	21	1	803
8.	Ipswich Town	42	650	1	16	0	815
9.	Derby County	42	535	5	27	0	830
10.	Stoke City	42	581	5	20	1	831
11.	Everton	42	626	4	19	0	836
12.	Leeds United	42	560	2	27	1	865
13.	Middlesborough	42	632	4	19	1	867
14.	Wolverhampton W.	42	590	3	24	1	870
15.	Queens Park Rangers	42	596	6	25	0	876
16.	Luton Town	42	627	4	21	2	907
17.	West Ham United	42	629	6	27	0	929
18.	Arsenal	42	616	6	27	2	966
19.	Birmingham City	42	648	4	28	1	973
20.	Burnley	42	679	4	32	1	1044
21.	Manchester City	42	699	1	30	2	1054
22.	Chelsea	42	667	4	41	2	1147

. . . an alternative league table in *Foul* magazine.

. . . information in the *Daily Mirror*.

sorted out press relations after taking over from Alf Ramsey in July 1974. Brian James of the *Sunday Times* was at first critical: 'The thing, *the* thing, about Revie is that he is another Ramsey. . . . They have the same basic distrust of the press, giving their confidence to few reporters and withdrawing that trust if they feel in any way betrayed.' But four months later he wrote: 'After 10 years dealing with Sir Alf Ramsey . . . the press are thrilled with the new relaxed Revie.' Revie commented: 'I'm not conning the press, but I am trying to use them.'

Two or three newspapers do try to look in some detail behind the scenes, but such features are the exception to the rule. However at least one publication tried a different approach. One of the founders of *Foul* magazine explained the reason for setting it up:

'The conception of it was a fairly serious thing. Trying to look at football in an adult way, without being intellectual. And to take a critical look at the press and their function, and what they were doing and saying. *Foul* as a title, as a contrast to *Goal* and *Shoot*, seemed to symbolize it. The contrast between the seamier side which we all know exists, and the media practice of painting it all white.'

Though some of the articles in *Foul* were rather predictable and occasionally biased in their criticism of boardroom politics or dirty play, there was plenty of good sharp journalism on topics not usually looked at by the national press, and a refreshing tendency to take nobody's words at face value. Unfortunately, lack of money forced *Foul* to stop publication in June 1975 after 30 issues but there is some hope that it may revive.

Ancient rivalries—England and Scotland

'There's never a need to wind them up for England,' said Manager Willie Ormond, just before Scotland's 2–0 victory over England in 1974. There's certainly a noticeable contrast between the Scots team's determination to win, and ability to do so, against the 'old enemy', and their performance against other countries. Whatever loyalty Scots David Hay, Alfie Conn or Martin Buchan may feel towards their English Clubs and the country where they play most of their football, there's nothing that gives them greater motivation to win than the annual clash with 'the Sassenachs'. No wonder some of the Scots party were upset when God Save the Queen was used as their national anthem before the 1974 World Cup games.

'The invasion of the Scots' is a favourite battle-cry in the press whenever Scotland play at Wembley. In May 1975 the hysteria reached such proportions that the workers on the underground trains between central London and Wembley went on strike, leaving many supporters to walk or hitch-hike seven miles each way to get to the game. 'A quieter Saturday night than normal' reported the police after Scotland's heavy 5–1 defeat by England: certainly not all the Scots went about refreshing themselves in the traditional way.

Ancient rivalries—Rangers and Celtic

'Nobody speaking about Rangers and Celtic should avoid the question of religion. The Rangers football club isn't actually a football club. It's an anti-Catholic football club. Celtic, although it started as a Catholic charitable organization, was not particularly religious. It was Irish. It was a national organization rather than a religious organization; and they have no religious scruples. Many Protestants have played for Celtic Football Club, but never a Catholic ever played for Rangers.' Clifford Hanley, Glasgow writer

'Rangers like big, strong, powerful fellows, with a bit of strength and a bit of solidity in the tackle rather than the frivolous, quick-moving stylists like wee Jimmy Johnstone, small, frivolous, tiptoe through the tulips type of players who excite the people.' Willie Waddell, Rangers Manager

'In every industrial society there are elements of the working class that actually get demoralized by the circumstances of their lives. In Scotland a strong section of that demoralized people identify with Rangers or Celtic. If Rangers and Celtic didn't exist something else would have to be invented that would be an object round which these elements would polarize.' Jimmy Reid, trade union leader

'I'm not just part of Celtic, Celtic is part of me. After the game we discuss it. Monday we discuss it. Tuesday we discuss it. The night when the magazine comes out, on Wednesday, we discuss it. This goes on week after week after week, every season, League Cup, League, Scottish Cup, European Cup—you name it, we discuss it. It's just football, football all the time.' Ricky Jackson, Chairman, Glasgow Celtic Emerald Gorbals Supporters' Club

John Thomson, the brilliant young goalkeeper who played for Scotland in 1930, was the only Protestant in the Celtic team. The following conversation took place between him and another Celtic player during the half-time interval:
Thomson: The centre-forward's been calling me a papish bastard.
McGrory: Don't let that worry you, I get called that every week.
Thomson: That's all right for you, you are one.

A familar scene at Ibrox Park: Rangers supporters stop the game in violent fashion after Celtic score in the League Cup.

The Final day

The Cup Final itself doesn't often produce outstanding football. But perhaps that doesn't matter very much. It's really more of a festival, a chance for people to celebrate the success of their team, to make sure the outside world knows that they exist—at least for a few days. And though the money boys move swiftly in on the two finalists and on the communities from which they come, the day of the Final still belongs to the supporters. The FA recently recognized who was really in charge, when they dropped the organized community singing which had been a pre-match tradition for as long as anyone can remember. Not many supporters can get enthusiastic about singing 'The Happy Wanderer' or even 'Abide with Me' when they have their own songs.

The Cup Final is probably the nearest thing we have to the village and street games of centuries past. It's also one of the occasions when the excitement spreads beyond the regular addicts, so that whole families, blocks of flats and streets get drawn into the celebration.

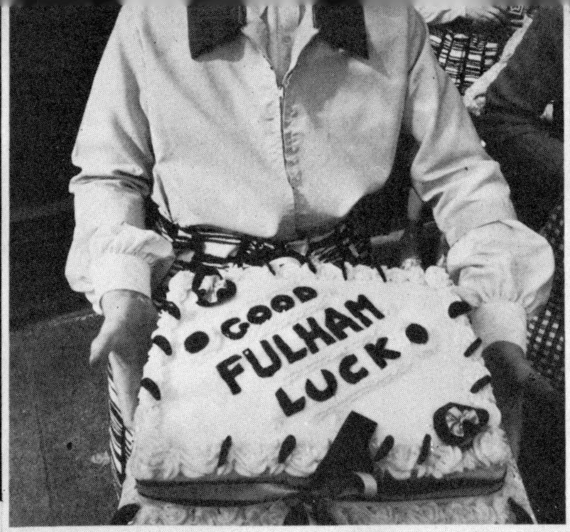
GOOD
FULHAM
LUCK

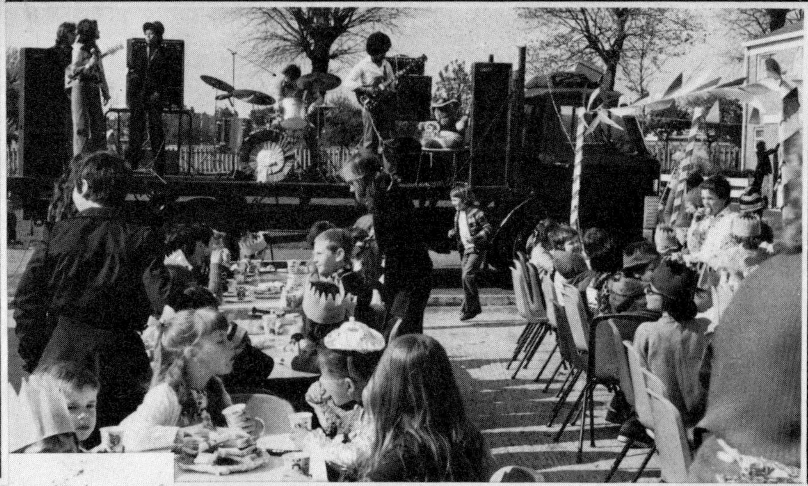

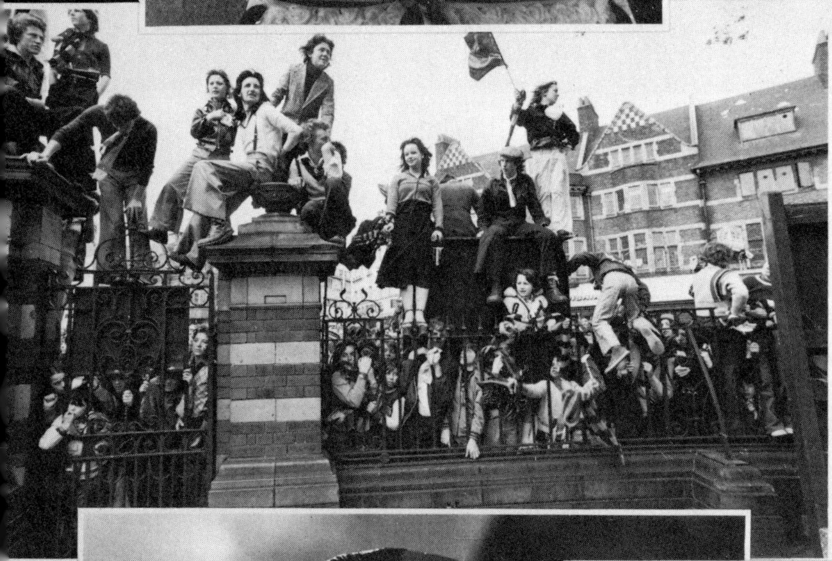

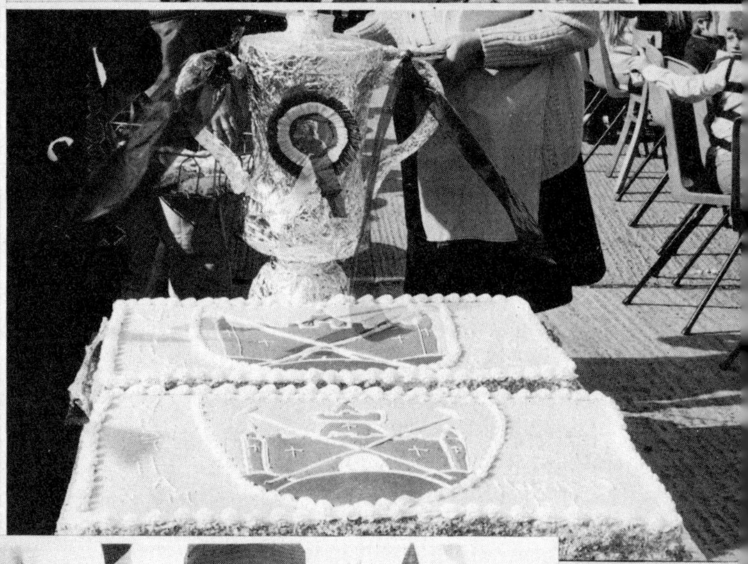

LUCK FULHA

WEST HAM
F.A.
CUP
FINALISTS
WEST HAM
F.A.Cup Final

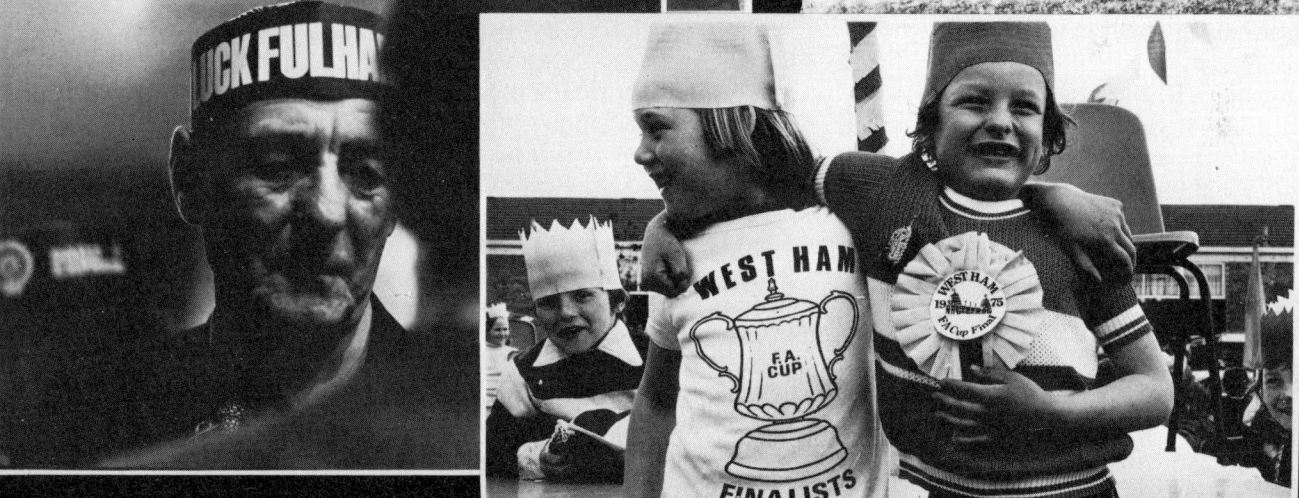

Keep right on

'I have an instinct to do the wrong things. That's probably my secret.' Johan Cruyff, Barcelona and Holland

Much of this book examines what is wrong with football. Maybe it is worth looking at the darker, hidden side of things, to supply some information and a few starting points for coming to more realistic conclusions about the game.

Let's not forget, though, that the well-publicized professional game is only the top of a pyramid, that broadens out into a fantastically wide base down amongst the village, works and even street teams that turn out every weekend. Football at this level is still enjoyed, whatever may be happening in the Football League or the FA Cup. It is this type of game which lies in the direct tradition of the early village games which inflamed whole villages from time to time.

And even now, when money, transport and other factors have broken the link between paid players and their communities, there is still room for the occasional upsurge of violent enthusiasm and delight when a lesser team conquers one of the heavyweights. Sunderland's victory over Leeds in the Cup in 1973 led to thousands of exiled Geordies returning to Sunderland for the weekend, remembering suddenly where they 'really belonged'.

The air may be heavy with rumours of financial collapse, part-time players in the League, sharp practice in the boardroom, and so on. At the international level football has certainly become subservient to political and commercial interests. But as long as skill, unpredictability and humour remain in the game, it is pretty likely to be played and watched by millions for quite a time yet.

Cup Final, 2072

Jack Rosenthal

Next Saturday, London United and Arts' Council-sponsored New Accrington Stanley will grace the polyester-fibre turf of Wembley for the 200th F.A. Cup Final.

Already the match is a sell-out. A capacity crowd of 27 is expected in the Sentimental Spectators' Enclosure – over and above the 988 million who'll be watching on TV, both on earth and in the Stretford End Penal Colony on the moon.

Unfortunately, the TV audience won't include several million viewers in Asia, engrossed in their own transmission of the vital bottom-of-the-table struggle between Crystal Palace and Peking Albion, now managed by veteran Tommy Docherty. (Until Wednesday, when he joins Antarctic Thistle until Friday.)

But, for the rest of us, Wembley promises perhaps the purest exhibition of football skill since the Peter Storey Prize for Gentlemanly Behaviour was introduced in the late 1970s.

A quick glance at the teams shows us why.

London United will be skippered by the only white player in the team, George Eastham – believed by pundits to be now actually